PAINTING DRAGONS

What Storytellers
Need to Know About
Writing Eunuch Villains

Tucker Lieberman

Copyright © 2018 Glyph Torrent (Bogotá, Colombia)

Cover art and design by Andi Santagata.

All rights reserved. This book or any portion thereof may not be reproduced or used in any manner whatsoever without the express written permission of the publisher except for the use of brief quotations in a book review or scholarly journal.

First printing (paperback): November 2018

["About the Author" was amended in 2020.]

ISBN-13: 978-1-7329060-1-3

CONTENTS

Introduction	What Color Is Your Dragon?	1
One	A European Tradition of Stereotypes	29
Two	Anxieties in Imperial China	48
Three	Representations of Persia	67
Four	Seekers of Revenge	95
Five	Sociopath, Vampire, Demon	110
Six	Meanings in Modern Empire	130
Seven	Not Evil Enough	142
Conclusion	Mirroring Magic	150
	Acknowledgments	159
	About the Author	160
	Bibliography	161

INTRODUCTION
WHAT COLOR IS YOUR DRAGON?

You're writing a story. One of your characters is a villain, and you're thinking of adding that he is a eunuch—that is, a castrated man. Or maybe it's the other way around: one of your characters is a eunuch, and you're thinking of adding that he is a villain. This color combination seems intriguing. It may yield an appealing story, and such a narrative may help readers comprehend themes like trauma and evil. The metaphor of castration may allow readers to explore topics that are emotionally intense and shrouded in shame. Why not go there?

Here's one reason you may want to hold back: The "eunuch villain" is an established trope. Castrated men have been typecast in novels as thoroughly evil: scheming, vengeful, indifferent to others' feelings. Any eunuch character, simply by being marked as a eunuch, can trigger this stereotype in the reader's imagination. He's a recognizable "color" in the artistic sense (as well as likely also drawing on some assumptions about race). His existence in your story will prompt readers to ask whether he'll turn out to fit the mold and why it is worth taking interest in him.

Before you decide how to write your character, it would be good to look at other stories where such characters have been done before. That's what this book, *Painting Dragons*, does. This is a deep dive into the stereotype of the evil eunuch in fiction.

I'm going to point out characters in fiction, their most salient traits, the common threads that join them, and what they mean from my perspective today. They might mean something very different to you. It will be an interesting experiment to keep not just an open *mind* about what really might exist (past, present, and future) but an open *imagination* about what those things could mean and how they could be portrayed artistically. By uncovering personalities that have already been written, you, as a writer, can make more informed choices about how to create new characters.

Why I Began Reading About Eunuchs

I am a transgender man, by which I mean that I was born female and decided to change my body and live as a man. My experience of masculinity is thus different from the norm. I was socialized as a girl, and my body is in some ways dissimilar from other men's bodies.

If people do not know this about me, they may wonder why I may seem a little different from other men. If, on the other hand, they are aware of my gender history, they may have some expectations about how a transgender man should behave, and I might not meet those expectations. This is a general truism about how stereotypes operate: they are always in our minds, whether or not we are conscious of them, whether or not they are based on fact, and whether or not it makes sense to apply them.

    I happen to have given a bit of thought to my own gender and to the way in which I live inside and outside certain molds. Because of that, I am positioned to empathize with eunuch characters in fiction, at least to the extent possible given that I am not one. When a novelist points out a character's gender as "eunuch," it is typically because that gender yields some conflict, challenge, special treatment, or strategic advantage or disadvantage within the story. I have a personal frame of reference for understanding some of those themes. I have the perspective of someone who has experienced a gender transformation of my own and who is consequently part of a marginalized gender minority.

    I am not, however, a eunuch, and it is important that I say so as I write this book. I have deeply invested myself in an eclectic reading list of fiction and nonfiction in which eunuchs are represented, but I am not (neither by physical embodiment nor by some other claim to identity) exactly the type of person who is being represented in those stories.

    Why did I begin reading fiction about eunuchs and not about transgender men? In part, it was due to my timing. I transitioned to a new gender as a teenager in the late '90s when there were fewer books about transgender identity and they were difficult to find. While I knew of a few nonfiction titles (clinical, political, memoir), I yearned for the kind of truths that are more commonly and more powerfully conveyed through narrative. I hadn't yet been exposed to many strong, mythic interpretations of gender-crossing people, certainly not as many as I personally wanted and needed, and I hadn't yet lived long enough to give them the complex interpretations that would make them relevant to me. I didn't have stories or language with which to interpret myself and the specific way in which I felt different.

I didn't expect to find any stories about transgender men in fiction, and, since I did not look for them, I did not find them. What I found, instead, were eunuchs, and they immediately captured my attention.

In college, I found a handful of such books, mostly by Western authors, on the library shelf. Initially, I encountered these characters primarily as harem guards in the Ottoman and Chinese empires, devotees to non-Christian gods, early Christian heretical monks, and Italian soprano singers. These are the ways they are most frequently known in the popular consciousness, at least in the books to which I had access.

Something about these descriptions appealed to me: sadness, hopelessness, unrelenting otherization. That was the way I understood myself at the time. I, too, presented as a man but, to my chagrin, I did not have a standard set of male genitalia. I had chosen to become infertile, which pleased me, but I was also aware of how infertility placed me outside what was often considered a normal or typical life plan. I had chosen this path, and the world would always see me as "other."

Eunuchs like the ones in my reading material really existed in the Roman, Chinese, and Persian empires. The reasons for their castrations, however, had begun to vanish into history, as had the social understanding that they belonged to a separate gender. Sun Yaoting, the last survivor of those eunuchs who served imperial China, died in 1996, just a couple years before I began to comb the library bookshelves at my university. Eunuchs were already socially extinct, or nearly so. That isn't to say that castration doesn't happen today, but it is to say that it typically happens in different ways, for different reasons, and that it is understood differently. There is not a eunuch gender role in exactly the way there used to be; it isn't common and it isn't obvious.

In the real world, as a human rights matter, this change is undoubtedly for the better. The end of slave systems that required castration means that boys are less likely to be mutilated in medically unsanitary, emotionally traumatic conditions and that adult men in desperate straits do not feel forced to submit to castration as a solution to their career problems. The end of widespread social endorsement of the idea of a "eunuch slave" is part of overall historical narratives about the abolition of slavery.

I hold this moral opinion about *actual abuse*, but, when I approached literature with a private agenda to interpret my gender, I had mixed feelings about the end of the widespread social *understanding* of "eunuch." The disappearance of collective awareness that eunuchs ever existed seemed to imply a diminished awareness of the history of masculinity.

The 20th century saw eunuch identity fall into obscurity just as transgender identity was rising. The existing fiction about eunuch characters was becoming less obvious in its original meaning and less relevant to modern life, and fiction about transgender characters hadn't yet fully emerged. I was part of a new medical and psychological category of people whose stories weren't yet interpreted on library shelves.

Although science fiction and fantasy have always

been replete with gender-bending experiences, I didn't begin with that literature. Either I couldn't easily find it or, perhaps because its universes were wholly imaginary, I didn't perceive it as describing my life or speaking to me. The characters I personally gravitated to, then, were eunuchs. To me, they seemed anchored in the real world such that they might guard clues about my own identity and purpose, yet also vanished from the real world such that I could permit myself the freedom to interpret them as symbols.

This was helpful, as it cleared a path to do my own imaginative inner work. There were several reasons for this.

First, since the eunuch gender category had mostly passed into history, I could view fictional eunuchs in some private metaphorical capacity without risking stepping on the physical toes of anyone I might meet on the street. I could *use* these characters imaginatively because they were about as distant as possible from real, living people. I didn't fear that I would offend others.

Second, if eunuchs were villainized or behaved in a disappointing manner, that characterization didn't step on *my* toes. I wasn't forced to read it as a direct commentary on or indictment of my own gender. I might feel a bit uncomfortable with the way characters were handled, but I didn't have to feel pained or enraged. I could step back and entertain mere curiosity about how the story might be *indirectly* relevant to me. This was a side benefit of not having many *directly* relevant stories about my actual gender. Some men prefer to read stories about men, some women prefer to read stories about women, and I—since I couldn't easily find representations of transgender men—had to learn to tolerate and benefit from more extended metaphors. I learned to identify with characters who seemed externally different from myself but with whom I shared some core motivation or perspective on a particular question.

Third, since it wasn't obvious that anyone alive today (in my own group or any other group) would be directly hurt by characterizations of eunuchs, I didn't feel an ethical responsibility to answer malign characterizations with immediate political action. I could think about the writer's intent and the result, but I didn't have to know the answer. Eunuch characters made fiction seem, to me, more of a playground than a political arena. It was a test space for ideas about gender where I could passively observe and explore my own intuitions without having to argue.

But it was also frustrating, because first-person eunuch narratives weren't often preserved and these people no longer existed to tell their stories of bygone times. I could never fully map their stories onto my own life story, nor my life onto theirs. (This challenge is perhaps faced more generally by readers of historical fiction.) Reading eunuch characters made me feel as if they reflected me, but only vaguely. I felt as if I were seen, but only in an abstract way, perhaps as a mythological being, not as a real person on the ground. I had a place in story but not necessarily in public life.

Therefore, no matter how much of this material I read or contemplated, I never felt *better*. I learned more about how themes and images functioned within literature, but I never learned exactly what eunuch characters could do for me or exactly why I was drawn to them. The existence of these characters acknowledged problems of gender and sexuality, but their disappearance from the real world meant that the questions they'd raised remained unresolved. I rarely felt I had tools to interpret the problem and bring those learnings back to real life. Contemplation simply amplified the problem, reminding me of my difference and discomfort.

Fiction—in contrast to nonfiction—shines in its ability to represent what remains unknown and difficult to grasp. This is also its weakness, as a novelist may dwell on whatever most resists explanation. In fiction, people with disabilities and physical quirks are often shown "as fathomless mysteries," according to David T. Mitchell and Sharon L. Snyder in their work of literary criticism *Narrative Prosthesis: Disability and the Dependencies of Discourse,* "who simultaneously provoke and elude cultural capture."[1] That is, the disabled character's very existence is shown as if begging for an analysis that no one can ever quite provide. Most stories don't get around to *asking* "whether disability is cause or symptom of, or distraction from, a disturbing behavioral trait," much less do they get around to *answering* that question.[2]

In accounts of eunuchs—including mythological interpretation, travel narratives by Westerners, and fiction informed by those writings—some authors were more credible than others, I gradually came to understand. Some had odd beliefs and prejudices about race, religion, gender, and sexuality, or they uncritically quoted others who did, thus conveying misperceptions to me and other readers. Some historical fiction was

---

[1] David T. Mitchell and Sharon L. Snyder. *Narrative Prosthesis: Disability and the Dependencies of Discourse.* Ann Arbor: The University of Michigan Press, 2000. [Kindle, 2014.] p. 61, 64.
[2] Mitchell and Snyder, p. 6.

more carefully researched than "nonfiction." Some patterns did not reveal truths but rather stereotypes. As I gradually realized that a book often says more about its author than about its subject, I began to take interest in the stereotypes the authors leveraged. I was interested in their mistakes of commission and omission: their deliberate portrayals as well as everything they left out.

I kept thinking that if I read "one more book" about eunuchs I'd finally spot the code and crack it open—as when, in response to continuous prayer, the angels respond in choral harmony, the answer is immediately revealed, and all pain is gone—but no such revelation was forthcoming. The eunuch code remained hidden. The eunuch *is* the code, this I intuited, but I didn't know how this could be or what it meant. The eunuch is the mystery who, paraphrasing Mitchell and Snyder, provokes and eludes his own capture.

Who Is a Eunuch Today?

While the famous eunuch slave systems are no longer in place and women are free to sing soprano roles, men are castrated today for a variety of other reasons. The most common reason is as a medical treatment for advanced prostate cancer. Male sex hormones fuel the growth of prostate cells, so doctors often recommend stopping the production of these hormones. About a half-million men living in North America today are on drugs that suppress their male hormones to a level that amounts to chemical castration. Because such drugs are expensive, surgical castration is used in places where access to the drugs is limited.[3]

Less frequently, men choose castration in an attempt to rid themselves of unwanted sexual urges. A few men have religious beliefs that spur them to do this, and some jurisdictions offer castration as a treatment for convicted sex offenders.[4] Other men incorporate castration into their sexual desires (sadomasochism or fetishism). Others, still, have a sense of "wrongness" about their body and express the need to castrate themselves to achieve what they feel will be a "normal" body for them. This psychological presentation has been variously labeled as Body Integrity Identity Disorder (BIID), xenomelia, or apotemnophilia.[5] It is hard to get accurate counts of any of these groups because they may not want to identify nor to be perceived as "eunuchs" nor to be classified under uncommon, pathologizing labels.

These days, castration usually does not affect someone's public identity. The English word "eunuch" is more often intended in a derogatory manner to imply that a man is a powerless pawn, not to describe his biological condition.

There are, of course, transgender women who may

---

[3] "On the invisibility of the emasculated." Guest editorial by Richard Wassersug. *Anthropology Today*. Feb. 2010. Vol 26, No. 1. pp. 1-3. For more information on this topic, see: Richard J. Wassersug, Lauren Walker, and John Robinson. *Androgen Deprivation Therapy, Second Edition: An Essential Guide for Prostate Cancer Patients and Their Loved Ones*. Demos, 2018.

[4] In the United States, when a convicted sex offender is offered this treatment option, he must consent to it; he cannot be sentenced to it against his will.

[5] Sedda A, Bottini G. Apotemnophilia, body integrity identity disorder or xenomelia? Psychiatric and neurologic etiologies face each other. Neuropsychiatr Dis Treat. 2014; 10: 1255–1265.

seek to feminize their bodies hormonally or surgically. It is important to realize that individuals who consider themselves women do not typically use words like "eunuch" or "castration" to describe themselves or their personal process.[6] I simply want to acknowledge here that transgender women exist and also to explain that, because this book explores notions of masculinity, I mostly exclude transgender women from consideration in this book. The concepts I use here probably do not directly apply to them and would likely result in misunderstandings or misrepresentations of their lives.

This is especially true for transgender women in India today, about whom I would like to make an additional comment. A longstanding cultural tradition in India allows people initially assigned a masculine role to live in a feminine role instead. Some of them were born intersex.[7] In many cases, they live communally with each other, and they are known within Hindu culture as performers at life cycle events. A variety of terms (including "eunuch") may be heard in popular discourse to describe these people, but that is often not the best term to use for them, as they usually prefer other words, some of which may be in their own languages and may not have English translations. Different individuals prefer different terms, understand themselves differently, and live in different ways. Since the experiences of these individuals in

---

[6] This term is complicated in India today. In the West, however, 20th- and 21st-century transgender women have not used the term "eunuch" nor been referred to that way.

[7] The word "intersex" describes people who are born with physical characteristics that aren't obviously female or male or that may combine traits of each.

India are generally dissimilar from those of the fictional, masculine eunuchs I discuss in this book, and since people who are alive today in large numbers with a robust culture can speak for themselves on issues that concern them, I have not pulled them into this book on fictional villains.

In various places, it might be possible to find a few individuals who personally embrace the term "eunuch." Most, of course, are not evil, nor do they necessarily conform to any other stereotype. They are people with whom it would be nice to share a cup of tea. They might even want to share opinions on literary villains.

Accepting what one is and what one is not is a first step toward connecting harmoniously with others. As a reader, I value challenging myself and widening my horizons, and my identity determines what it means for me to challenge myself and which of my horizons need to be widened. As a writer, my work is subject to others' decisions about whose work they will read.

My identity has many parts. I am a white, American, atheist, Jewish, college-educated, liberal, secular humanist, gay, transgender man. I am able-bodied and of average weight. I am English-speaking with reading knowledge of several languages. I am in a same-sex marriage. I have a U.S. passport and a Colombian identity card that says I am an immigrant. Over the course of my life, my identity has contributed to what I was encouraged to read and write, what I thought I wanted to read and write, and what I was open to reading and writing.

When you write a story about eunuchs, it's good to think about who might identify with that label as well as who might not. Some people who aren't castrated males may nonetheless feel some kinship with eunuchs. Some people who are castrated males may dislike the term "eunuch" and want nothing to do with the idea. Either kind of person may be affected by your book. They can be affected directly, if they happen to obtain a copy of your book, or indirectly, by the images and messages you have spread into the world.

What Makes a Villain?

We all have to be able to recognize the villain. Whatever the villain is doing in a story, his negative object lesson can serve as a backbone for others' ethical formation.

Learning what we're "not supposed to do" is part of our earliest childhood awareness. Even within advanced ethical study, we often have to pay attention to the vice before we can understand the corresponding virtue that offsets it. We have to be able to spot (for example) greed, entitlement, and arrogance before we can fully cultivate generosity, gratitude, and humility.

The villain is the guy in the movie who ties the lady to the railroad tracks, Chuck Klosterman explains in *I Wear The Black Hat: Grappling With Villains (Real and Imagined)*. This has been a melodramatic trope for over a hundred years. It's as old as trains. The villain twists his mustache, binds the hapless woman to tracks in a deserted area, rubs his hands gleefully, and cackles as he waits for the locomotive to arrive. (The dramatic delay provides opportunity of rescue.) "It's almost as if the concept of using a train to kill someone is so complicated and absurd," Klosterman writes, "that it can only be viewed as a *caricature* of villainy. It was never based on any legitimate fear."[8]

It doesn't appeal to a fear of homicide-by-train, perhaps. But it must appeal to some fear or it wouldn't be a credible tale of villainy. Evil characters are atavistic; that is, they manifest traits of some long-forgotten ancestor.[9] The fictional villain is created to express an underlying concern—like, for example, the fear of a man confining a woman by elaborate means simply because it pleases him to do so. That's something that really happens.

A villain brings certain themes into sharp relief. He can be drunk on power, crazy, or simply emotional. In Shakespeare's plays, writes David McNally in *Monsters of the Market: Zombies, Vampires and Global Capitalism,* we hear about "'monstrous envy' and 'monstrous lust' *(Pericles),* 'monstrous arrogance' *(The Taming of the Shrew)* and 'monster ingratitude' *(King Lear).* Perhaps no emotion figures more ominously than jealousy, which the poet describes in *Othello* as 'the green-eyed monster'."[10] Obsession and revenge (and obsessive revenge!) are among the popular motives for villains,[11] especially concerning someone who was castrated against his will. Such a narrow, intense psychological response by a eunuch tends to make intuitive sense to readers.

---

[8] Klosterman, p. 10.

[9] Matt Kaplan writes: "Called atavisms, these genetic mutations can create chimeric-looking organisms. But atavisms are not totally random in what they do. They do not simply grant a random trait. Humans are not born with wings and snakes are not born with fur. Instead, they produce traits that existed in the evolutionary past of that animal." Kaplan, p 36.

[10] McNally, p. 63.

[11] Ferguson, Jelke, Morgan, Plemmons, and Sylvestre, "Chapter 2: Archetypes," p. 23.

Managing fears through fiction is also common. People watch horror films, Stephen T. Asma writes in *On Monsters: An Unnatural History of Our Worst Fears*, to release "pent-up pressures" and "anxiety in a cathartic manner," and people buy horror merchandise because "commodifying a horror is one way of objectifying and managing it."[12] Some people find that recreational horror makes them feel more stressed and vulnerable, but others find it relaxing and reassuring.

If a villain dies quickly and decisively, we can feel sadness and regret with a sense of the tragic; if he cannot be killed and lingers mysteriously despite everyone else's best intentions and efforts, we are filled with dread.[13]

Most people have some fascination with danger and violence. If we don't enjoy subjecting ourselves to the real thing, we still may occasionally contemplate or admire it in fiction or film. This may be "part of our furnished mind," an evolutionary inheritance, following Asma's observation of a "wonderfully ambivalent tension in Darwin's zoo monkeys. The monkey cannot fully confront the snake, but he cannot leave it alone either. He is repelled and attracted."[14]

Not all risks are in the realm of human evil. The

---

[12] Asma, pp. 196, 197, 280.

[13] Steven Church writes: "I can't help but feel sorry for the bear. I don't want her to die, but I know she has to for the sake of the movie. I know that it makes a better story if the monster dies and the hero survives. It makes the story a tragedy. But part of me wants the typical horror movie trope where she rises from the dead, lets out a monstrous roar, and savagely mauls three or four other men before finally dying at Glass's hand." Church, p. 19. Although Church wrote about an animal, the same lesson may apply to humans who are seen as dangerously immoral or amoral.

[14] Asma, p. 4.

adrenaline rush we feel when we are in danger or when we see someone else in danger probably predates moral concepts and can be felt in non-moral situations. A large, hungry animal may inspire a sense of the holy fear we call the sublime. "The bear is never just a bear," says Steven Church in his 2016 book *One With the Tiger: Sublime and Violent Encounters Between Humans and Animals*. Church's book also explores the impulse by one man to physically intimidate or hurt another man as part of his sense of masculinity. The bear, he says, "is always something greater and more wild, more sublime and powerful than humans can perhaps ever fully understand."[15] Any external threat, then, even an amoral one, may raise questions about our own identity and power.

Seeing human intention behind the danger adds an extra layer of complexity. Human survival depends, in part, on defeating human evil. The battle is often partly internal, as we resist facing our own malign tendencies, including anger, fear, hate, cruelty, ignorance, indifference, and other auxiliary forces to evil. We usually prefer to combat an external foe than to identify ourselves as the problem.

When the Eunuch Is the Villain

The eunuch is probably most famous for guarding women in the harem. In various cultures and imperial systems, young women in particular were kept with the obligation to serve the sexual needs of a man and to produce heirs for him. Popular culture remembers the eunuch's assignment as a harem guard because it seems to make logical sense out of his castration. Due to his

---

[15] Church, p. 34.

intermediate sexual status, he was given permission to travel between men's and women's quarters and also into public space, while women's travel was often restricted. The eunuch was thus in a position to be a security escort for women, to arrange for their daily needs, and to report back to men about women's health and pregnancy status. Like the women he guarded, the eunuch was considered a servant or slave, even if he became a powerful one. A concubine's life was forfeit if she attempted to escape, or if she was caught sexually compromised, or for no reason at all. An unpleasant fate was always possible for the eunuch, too, if he was corrupt, allowed women to misbehave, displeased someone, or was discovered never to have been properly castrated. His life could also be dispatched at the sovereign's command.

The harem woman was tied down, metaphorically. She was trapped by at least one man or eunuch, and she may have hoped for another man or eunuch to rescue her.

Tying someone to the railroad tracks, then, is not only "a caricature of *villainy*" (to shift the emphasis on Klosterman's phrase). It's possible for someone to see in the railroad tracks, more specifically, a caricature of the *harem*. It's the place where someone is tied down. If the tracks are the harem, that makes the cackling, hand-rubbing man (despite his iconic facial hair) a caricature of the *eunuch*.

It is possible that the truer villain in a harem was the man who was master of the house and who controlled eunuchs and women alike and that the eunuch was a tool in the situation, more analogous to the rope used for tying up others. But the eunuch, not the man, was the controlling personality who more frequently directly interacted with women. The eunuch was often the human face put on women's captivity.

At the same time as monsters "reflect the fears of specific eras," Asma writes, "they also reflect more universal human anxieties and cognitive tendencies."[16] Eunuchs have, at times, been considered outright monsters, a theme that will recur throughout this book.

People have always felt anxiety about eunuchs. Women, in certain times and places, have had reason to fear how eunuchs might be employed to restrict their freedom. Men often felt a lurking anxiety about whether a eunuch was "real" or "false," the "false eunuch" being another ancient literary trope referring to a man who disguised himself to sneak into women's quarters.[17] Today, at least, transgender people generally dislike being misinterpreted as eunuchs; we also dislike when our gender transition is interpreted as a kind of disguise.[18] And men, of course, are often anxious about

---

[16] Asma, p. 283.

[17] Refer to the Chinese history of Lao Ai in the 3rd century BCE, and also to the Roman play "Eunuchus" by Terence in the 2nd century BCE which is said to be based on a Greek fragment "Eunouchos" by Menander in the 4th century BCE.

[18] The most recent, prominent instance of linking transgender identity with disguise—at least the one that comes to my mind—is a referendum in my home state of Massachusetts. As of this writing, the November 2018 vote is still a few weeks away. With this referendum, a group is challenging an existing state law that currently allows each individual to choose the public bathroom (men's or women's) that the individual feels best corresponds to his or her own gender identity. The opposition's argument for repealing the law is not that transgender people are dangerous, but that *dangerous men might disguise themselves as transgender women* to access women's spaces with intent to assault women. They speculate that this elaborately villainous threat demands a preemptive legislative response, even though they cannot cite a

the possibility that they could be castrated, which is a painful physical event that carries long-term biological and social consequences. Most men fear losing their sexual libido, their fertility, their masculine self-image, their social standing with other men, and their gender privilege in public life. They may also be attached to the belief that their testicles provide some essential support to their personality and character. All of these anxieties lend partial explanation for why eunuchs are so easily vilified.

Because we are taught that our genitals (and how we choose to treat them) reflect our character, it is no surprise that castration is often taken to represent vice and shame, and that intact genitalia would then seem to be badges of honor. Reflecting upon and articulating this idea reveals it as an illusion. The idea that uncastrated people are better than castrated ones is a self-serving assumption that helps some people feel better about themselves but cannot cast accurate judgment on anyone's character.

More generally, noticing bodies that have been affected by injury or illness or that do not correspond to some expectation or ideal tends to prompt awareness of our own mortality and vulnerability. Being aware of our physical vulnerability is a survival skill, but this awareness can easily slide into a

---

single instance of such an attempt. The "danger" is entirely imaginary. The idea of a "false transgender woman" evokes the older literary trope of a "false eunuch"—well, it evokes that notion for me, anyway. The point is, it's all fiction. Transgender people aren't in disguise for nefarious purposes, and people who suggest that we are in disguise are often attempting to take away basic rights pertaining to our gender identity, like our ability to choose an appropriate bathroom without being questioned or harassed.

superiority complex hinging on how our bodies happen to fit whatever standard we are using to judge ourselves.

The eunuch thus ends up in popular imagination as a villain, a sort of caricature of himself. Seeing a eunuch's beardless face or hearing his high voice may cause some people to feel uncomfortable. Maybe the one who feels uncomfortable is also beardless and strange-voiced, or used to be, or realizes that he could become so someday. We push away, "otherize," or even demonize what we are afraid to accept in ourselves. This contributes to depictions of eunuch villains. As long as there is real anxiety about him, fiction is an exercise with which the reader tests and conquers anxiety.[19]

If You Are Considering Writing About Eunuchs

If you're thinking of putting a eunuch in your story, it may be because you have a stereotype of what a eunuch is supposed to be or do. Character stereotypes and plot tropes can be based on accurate information or personal experience but still can be harmful or counterproductive. If your reader recognizes the recycled image, the story may fall flat aesthetically for them and, in their eyes, you can lose credibility as an author.

This book has several examples of the stereotype. In these examples, the castrated man is always a villain

---

[19] Matt Kaplan writes: "To a certain extent, danger should function as the life essence of monsters. Once a perceived danger is dispelled, this essence is destroyed and the beast becomes extinct. It may continue to live on in fiction as a fossil of its former self or as a mere creature of interest, but not as a monster with all of the terror that comes with such status." Kaplan, p. 6.

(a stereotype in itself), and he may also be dark-skinned, Eastern, obese, or mentally or physically disabled; all are possible components of the trope.

What are the consequences of repeating this stereotype? It may limit how innovative the story can be in showing how a character can evolve and what the story can accomplish in helping real people interpret themselves. By presenting such a person as a villain, you may imply that these characteristics are *overriding*, now and forever. You may imply that they *warp* someone's character and *define* it. This may convey (even if only accidentally) more general beliefs about the limitation of human potential.

Nisi Shawl and Cynthia Ward address this in their 2005 manual *Writing The Other: A Practical Approach*. They explain that, because some characteristics (including gender, sexuality, race, and ability) are more common, probable, or privileged than others, many readers tend to assume that a character has a set of default traits (e.g. male, heterosexual, white, able-bodied) unless they specifically hear otherwise. People also tend to remember negative, prejudiced information about "marked states" of difference, "even when our conscious minds know the information is false."[20] Well-meaning writers, anxiously assuming it's bad to notice and point out differences, may want all their characters to exist in an "unmarked state." But this is not the best approach. Millions of men throughout history have been marked by castration, after all. Erasing them is not a solution. What's needed is a way to acknowledge a difference without having that difference dominate and

---

[20] Shawl and Ward, chap. 2.

determine the character's entire life.

A character's disability, injury or marginalized status does not have to turn them into a monster, nor in any other respect need it take center stage. A physically or socially limiting condition can be understood in the rich context of a normal, complete human life. When literature is well executed, it can give readers tools to see humanity with more richness and nuance; poorly executed, it can oversimplify and reduce the human experience.

Some literary critics have shown how the portrayal of constrained life options for disabled people, especially the effects of social isolation, often assumes that those constraints are "inevitably leading toward bitterness and anger." Whether a disabled character is seen as a hero often depends on their "ability to adjust to or overcome their tragic situation" or to persist in living "within a drama of [their] own making."[21] The social context of how others might need to change or how a system might need to change is often not considered.

Some stories about eunuchs—both fiction and nonfiction—stick in readers' imaginations because they have memorably prurient details. A boy may be kidnapped, drugged with opium, given a warm bath, washed with extract of hot pepper as a local anesthetic, see a large curved knife, have his urethra plugged with metal, and be buried in hot desert sand for three days. He may then be sold to a family, given a new name and a new costume, and learn the protocols of eunuch servants. He may be publicly recognizable as a eunuch because of his voice, accent, skin, height, weight, and

---

[21] Mitchell and Snyder, pp. 18-19.

general attitude and demeanor.

These are parts of typical narratives. They are based on historical accounts. The details may be shocking and may draw in readers. Readers' heightened interest, however, does not entail that they are learning important (nor even accurate) history.

As a writer of fiction, you know that you're projecting traits and problems onto imaginary characters so that your readers can more readily absorb and internalize these themes and relate the story to their own lives. Your readers, too, already recognize this as an important reason they read fiction. Regardless of whether you or your readers use terms like "projection" and "internalization," everyone intuits how stories work and how they affect us.

Evil characters present a special challenge. As journalist Rachel Martin said of fictional villains (referring to those who are sexual predators), they may appear "cartoonish" when there's not enough complex personal information to engage the reader and, on the other hand, they may appear "too sympathetic" if the reader is given opportunities to identify closely with them.[22] These worries about weaknesses in the story are not merely aesthetic. After all, if fiction intends to enlighten readers or to equip us for moral action, then what we are really worried about is our own moral character.

Projecting a cartoonish version of evil shuts down our ability to understand true evil or fully respond to

---

[22] Rachel Martin. "Depicting Sexual Predators As Villains In Fiction Is Tricky." Weekend Edition. NPR. Sept. 25, 2016. https://www.npr.org/2016/09/25/495358007/depicting-sexual-predators-as-villains-in-fiction-is-tricky Accessed August 20, 2018.

it. As long as we assume that evil looks obvious to us and entirely unlike us, it will always be unapparent to us (often hidden in plain sight) and we will tend to tolerate or even reproduce it. "[W]hat we do not understand at all," the philosopher Mary Midgley says in *Wickedness*, "we cannot detect or resist." On the other hand, when we begin to sympathize with someone else's evil, it feels like an uncomfortable acknowledgement that we have some of that evil capacity within ourselves. No matter whether that capacity was only recently drawn in or whether it was always there, it's self-damning to call it out. The necessary response to evil simultaneously requires a slow, cautious, deep *understanding* and a swift, bold, broad-brush *rejection*. These two requirements are in tension. To understand is, in some sense, to accept; to reject is, in some sense, to cease to understand. We must *provisionally* sympathize with evil so that we can at least understand what psychology we are rejecting, but this very moment of provisional sympathy, no matter how thin, taints and disturbs us.

In real-life disagreements, we often disallow ourselves and each other the opportunity to feel any moral sympathy with an enemy. In reading fiction, provisionally sympathizing with and understanding the villain's character is part of the point. How should we distance our minds from evil? How far is too far? How close is too close?

Fiction allows writers and readers to explore this moral conundrum playfully and with lower stakes, yet writers must still acknowledge that, in some measure, the story's ideas reflect or influence real life. Therefore, writers must pay attention to how they handle their villains and must make a good faith effort to portray them well. Negative traits will be projected onto the villain. One of the deciding factors in the success of this endeavor is how deliberate and self-aware this projection is. Usually we land on stronger moral ground when we are telling stories with conscious understanding of how they work. When we unconsciously project negative traits onto characters, we risk falling into and perpetuating stereotypes. The stereotypes we do not understand, to appropriate Midgley's idea, cannot be detected or resisted.

What Follows: A Walkthrough of the Most Villainous Eunuch Tales

This book focuses on novels in which the eunuch character is portrayed as unremittingly villainous. In some cases, I'll discuss these novels in full, including their endings.

I've excluded novels in which eunuch characters are treated as complex, normal humans or as having wise, heroic, or saintly traits. Such stories are interesting in their own right, but examining those different premises would require me (or someone else) to write a new, separate book.

Chapter 1 examines the treatment of Eutropius, a real Roman consul, in the satire *In Eutropium* by his 4th-century contemporary, the poet Claudian. It also looks at the treatment of Narses, a real 6th-century Byzantine general, in the novel *Count Belisarius* by a 20th-century English man. It ends with a discussion of the treatment of eunuchs within an early 18th-century screed, *Eunuchism Display'd*, published in French and English.

Chapter 2 looks at a fictional account of a 15th century Ming dynasty eunuch power-grab in Jeremy Han's *The Prisoners of Fate* (2015). It also reviews the fictional treatment of Wei Zhongxian, a real person in the later Ming dynasty in the 17th century, and the entirely imaginary farce of Li Pi Siao, the chief of the harem in Charles Pettit's *The Son of the Grand Eunuch* (1920).

Chapter 3 looks at stories of eunuchs based on Persian culture. These characters include Aga Mohamed Khan, a real ruler in the late 18th century, fictionalized by a British writer in *Zohrab, the Hostage* (1832); a eunuch chief of police in Dennis Wheatley's *The Eunuch of Stamboul* (1935); and a chief harem guard in Fiona McIntosh's fantasy land of Percheron in the trilogy *Odalisque, Emissary,* and *Goddess* (2005–2007).

Chapter 4 identifies two novels with identical premises and the same title, *The Last Castrato,* published in 1995 by John Spencer Hill and 2006 by J. Wolf Sanchez. In each, a boy soprano, castrated in Florence long after it was fashionable to do so, suffers emotional trauma and seeks revenge.

Chapter 5 focuses on tales in modern settings. Iain Banks' *The Wasp Factory* (1984) is narrated by a child on a Scottish island who becomes a young serial killer. John Ajvide Lindqvist's novel *Let Me In* (2004) features a child vampire. Dan Brown's *The Lost Symbol* (2009) is driven by a man who bears a grudge, decides he wants to become a demon, and stops at nothing to accomplish his transformation.

Chapter 6 looks at how the metaphor of the harem eunuch is used against transgender women in Janice Raymond's *The Transsexual Empire* (1994). It also looks at the parallels between "eunuchism" and "transsexualism" as drawn by Howard Chiang in *After Eunuchs* (2018).

Chapter 7 briefly examines stories with eunuch

characters whose malevolence is understated: Knut Hamsun's *The Women at the Pump* (1920), Gustave Flaubert's *Salammbo* (1862), and George R. R. Martin's ongoing saga *A Song of Ice and Fire* (1996 and onward). I've set apart these characters because I see them as merely creepy, unsettling, or compromised, and less obviously villainous, although others may have different interpretations.

This book's title, *Painting Dragons,* is inspired by the words of James Justinian Morier, the author of *Zohrab, the Hostage,* in his explanation of how he turned a real-life political tyrant into a villain for his novel. "I have placed him in my narrative," Morier prefaces his story, "as a painter sometimes inserts a dragon or some such monster in the foreground of his landscape."[23] He implies that writing a fictional villain is similar to painting a mythical beast and that the writer's choice may be dictated by personal preference for mainly aesthetic reasons. It is indeed a personal choice, but for that very reason it is important to recognize that different approaches can be taken. Eunuchs are real. Cruelty is real. Dragons are not real. We choose the dragons we paint.

Eunuch characters who are stereotypical, thoroughgoing villains may not be able to be rehabilitated in fiction. Remembering how avidly I once sought books about eunuchs, it's funny now to think about redeeming these characters, when I always wanted eunuch characters to redeem me. I don't think I can "save" the eunuch villain and turn him into something positive, I don't think he is going to save us, and I don't need to write him into new stories (though other

---

[23] Morier, Preface, p. vi.

writers might feel the need to do so). My goal is more modestly to examine him as he already exists. When we pay attention to how we look at a fictional character, we can then use that skill to turn the mirror around to face ourselves.

This is not to say that you, as a novelist, cannot write characters similar to those who have already been created. There may be room for more eunuch villains in fiction. I am of the opinion, however, that there is a greater current need for fictional eunuchs who *aren't* villains. When characters are one-dimensional and evil, it is hard to relate to them. Reading too many eunuch villains causes us to form literary stereotypes and deep unconscious associations about gender that we apply outside of the novel to other areas of life. The recurrence of eunuch villains in literature can spoil the wisdom-seeking quest for those readers who need a different message.

Once you are aware of the meaning of the eunuch villains discussed in the following pages, you should give yourself permission to create the characters you need, want, and choose to paint—and then accept responsibility for the color of your dragon.

CHAPTER ONE
A EUROPEAN TRADITION OF STEREOTYPES

Eutropius and Narses are among the most recognized names of ancient eunuchs. They were real people and, although this book will tend to avoid real people, it is worth considering how real people can be fictionalized. After discussing these individuals, I will then examine a work of 18th-century nonfiction that is notable and useful for fiction writers because it exposes ancient and contemporary stereotypes.

The Consul Eutropius

> ...many people seem to believe [incorrectly] that Hitler had only one testicle (and that this monarchism explains his diabolical nature). Some historians have spent years investigating this belief, and most conclude that it's an urban legend. But this is further evidence of Hitler's exceptionalism: I can't think of any other

> public figure whose scrotum feels historically meaningful (or disputed).
>
> Chuck Klosterman, *I Wear The Black Hat*[24]

> *omnia cesserunt eunucho consule monstra* (All prodigies have given way, when a eunuch is consul.)
>
> Claudian, *In Eutropium*, 399 CE[25]

Today, we know the eunuch Eutropius, who was appointed as a Roman consul, mainly through the satirical exaggeration of the contemporary poet Claudian. Claudian's literary hit job also has elements of an epic insofar as he shows the gods conversing with and interfering with humans. Not all events represent literal fact. (In one scene of the poem, the Roman goddess of war Bellona turns herself into a bird.) The exaggerated literary characterization of Eutropius makes him—even though he was a real person—an ancestor of fictional eunuch villains.

The poem *In Eutropium* ("Against Eutropius") was issued in two installments, and these together constitute about seven thousand Latin words of invective verse in dactylic hexameter, solely directed against one particular eunuch, largely because of his gender. Jacqueline Long says in her scholarly analysis *Claudian's In Eutropium: Or, How, When, and Why to Slander a Eunuch* that she counts fifty-eight references to Eutropius' "lack of virility."[26] In his day, eunuchs had served wealthy households for four hundred years in Rome and for twice as long in Greece. Basic cultural

---

[24] Klosterman, p. 190.
[25] *Eutr.* 1.8.
[26] Long, p. 107.

expectations about them were well established; nonetheless, Long wrote, they "did look abnormal, and their strangeness could be perceived as unpleasant."[27]

Originally serving Emperor Theodosius, Eutropius rose in the ranks of the palace eunuchs. Upon Theodosius' death in 395 CE, the Roman Empire split in two: his son Arcadius became emperor of the East and his son Honorius became emperor of the West.[28]

Eutropius continued to serve Emperor Arcadius. As his advisor and general, he achieved a military victory in 398 CE. He was honored with the rank of patrician and consul, but this was short-lived, for two reasons. First, Emperor Honorius took the rare action of refusing to recognize the rank that his brother Arcadius had assigned to Eutropius. Second, a rebel Roman general defeated Eutropius' forces and, primarily to mollify this rebel, Emperor Arcadius removed Eutropius from his position as consul and exiled him. The official declaration in 399 CE read that the consulate was "vindicated from the foul muck and from the commemoration of his name and its filthy stains."[29] Ultimately, Eutropius was executed.

The poet Claudian's first volley against Eutropius was written just after he was made consul but before this appointment had caused him misfortune. The poem was primarily a mockery of the very idea of a eunuch consul.

Whereas Chuck Klosterman says he can't recall a

---

[27] Long, p. 109.
[28] This was a fateful split that heralded the end of the Roman Empire. The East would eventually become known as the Byzantine Empire with its capital in Constantinople and Greek as its new official language, while the West would fizzle out.
[29] Theodosian Code 9.40.17

public figure aside from the infamous Nazi leader "whose scrotum feels historically meaningful,"[30] Eutropius' scrotum, if I may respond to Klosterman's implicit challenge, did matter. Claudian is prejudiced against both slaves and eunuchs: "Nothing is so cruel as a man raised from lowly station to prosperity," he writes in the poem, since "remembering his own master he hates the man he lashes."[31] To the poet, a eunuch seems worse than a normal man, as the eunuch was believed to be "moved by no natural affection" including family bonds.[32]

But Eutropius sinks beneath even the low bar set for him. His greed and cruelty are excessive beyond what is expected for a eunuch; he is abusive to his own kind, that is, to other eunuchs. His lust for money is "the only passion his mutilated body can indulge."[33] Eutropius supposedly sold political positions and jailed rivals, which alone would be a significant complaint, and in Claudian's depiction of him as sexually deviant, we hear a louder complaint that he is something other than fully human.

Look at how Claudian begins the first book, and you quickly get the idea:

---

[30] Klosterman, p. 190.
[31] *Eutr.* 1.181-186. ("Asperius nihil est humili cum surgit in altum:/cuncta ferit dum cuncta timet, desaevit in omnes/ut se posse putent, nec belua taetrior ulla/quam servi rabies in libera terga furentis;/agnoscit gemitus et poenae parcere nescit,/quam subiit, dominique memor, quem verberat, odit.")
[32] *Eutr.* 1.187-190. ("adde, quod eunuchus nulla pietate movetur/nec generi natisve cavet. clementia cunctis/in similes, animosque ligant consortia damni;/iste nec eunuchis placidus.")
[33] *Eutr.* 1.190-191. ("Sed peius in aurum/aestuat; hoc uno fruitur succisa libido.")

> Let the world cease to wonder at the births of creatures half human, half bestial, at monstrous babes that affright their own mothers, at the howling of wolves heard by night in the cities, at beasts that speak to their astonied herds, at stones falling like rain, at the blood-red threatening storm clouds, at wells of water changed to gore, at moons that clash in mid heaven and at twin suns. All portents pale before our eunuch consul.[34]

In simpler terms, this means: No supernatural horror could possibly be worse than a castrated man in power. Such a man, appearing as a human inversion of the natural order, will make Rome a magnet for divine punishment.

Supernatural beliefs were taken seriously in Rome, where, at this time in history, the Senate occasionally consulted the prophetic Sybilline Books for insight into difficult questions. Deformed infants were seen as bad omens. It was a legal obligation to kill them (as decreed in the fourth of the "Twelve Tables" of Roman Law that dated back to the 5th century BCE), and intersex children (those whose physical sex was ambiguous, known then as "hermaphrodites") were included in this group. Cases of infanticide of intersex children in the 2nd and 1st centuries BCE were documented by Livy, although this may have softened somewhat by the 1st century CE when Pliny described intersex people as "sources of entertainment."[35] This is the cultural context for calling a eunuch a bad omen. The Latin word *monstrum* ("monster") occurs eight times in

---

[34] *Eutr.* 1.1-8. This is Maurice Platnauer's 1922 translation from Latin to English.
[35] Asma, p. 41-42.

the two parts of the poem, and it means, literally, that the person functions as a warning (*monere*, "to warn").[36]

To avoid whatever terrifying fate is approaching, the narrator demands Eutropius' death: "the monster itself must be sacrificed."[37] In breathless hyperbole, he tells us that this situation "surpass[es] all that is most laughable in comedy, most lamentable in tragedy."[38]

Promote a slave to be consul, fine, says Claudian, "but at least give us a man."[39] And though a woman's rule would be illegal under Roman law, it would be "less disgraceful"[40] to Rome than a eunuch in government; ruling queens are known elsewhere, but "we know of no people who endure a eunuch's rule."[41] Indeed: "Never have we seen so much as a ship at sea obey the helm in the hands of a eunuch-captain."[42] It might be acceptable somewhere in the East, he says, but not in Rome.

When a man is castrated, he is "made for servitude."[43] Forgetting—or erasing—Eutropius' military victory, he asked: "What noble deed did a eunuch ever do? What wars did such an one fight, what

---

[36] Asma, p. 13. McNally, p. 9.
[37] *Eutr.* 1:19-22. ("quae tantas expiet iras/victima? quo diras iugulo placabimus aras?/consule lustrandi fasces ipsoque litandum/prodigio")
[38] *Eutr.* 1:298-299. ("exempla creantur/quae socci superent risus luctusque cothurni")
[39] *Eutr.* 1:29. ("da saltem quemcumque virum")
[40] *Eutr.* 1:320-321. ("sumeret inlicitos etenim si femina fasces/esset turpe minus")
[41] *Eutr.* 1:323-324. ("gens nulla probatur/eunuchi quae sceptra ferat")
[42] *Eutr.* 1:424-425. ("numquam vel in aequore puppim/vidimus eunuchi clavo parere magistri")
[43] *Eutr.* 1:332. ("hoc genus inventum est ut serviat")

cities did he found?"[44] Furthermore, he denies that eunuchs are represented among gods and priests, even though, earlier, in this very book, he acknowledges the myth of Tiresias[45] (a male prophet who, by an angry goddess' magic spell, was transformed into female form and lived as a woman for seven years until he reverted to male form) and the worship of the goddess Cybele[46] (whose real human devotees ritually self-castrated).

Claudian likens Eutropius to a woman and calls him a "half-man" (*semivir*).[47] He then disparages him as an *unwanted* eunuch: a sex slave who became tiresome, a disgraced servant passed between masters "anxious to rid their houses of him by...foist[ing] the loathsome gift on an unsuspecting friend"[48] or on slave markets, and a person reduced to pandering or pimping. Claudian says Eutropius is now shameless and ugly and is accordingly treated like an old, useless dog (*canem*).[49] Later, he's called an ape (*simius*).[50]

Long comments that he is depicted in feminine roles. As she puts it, he is shown as "a castoff mistress, an impotent whore, a sexless nurse, a bibulous mother-in-law, an overaged Amazon, and a hated taskmistress."[51]

---

[44] *Eutr.* 1:336-337. ("quid nobile gessit/eunuchus? quae bella tulit? quas condidit urbes?")
[45] *Eutr.* 1:315.
[46] *Eutr.* 1:277, 325.
[47] *Eutr.* 1:171.
[48] *Eutr.* 1:38-41. ("postquam deforme cadaver/mansit et in rugas totus defluxit aniles,/iam specie doni certatim limine pellunt/et foedum ignaris properant obtrudere munus.")
[49] *Eutr.* 1:133.
[50] *Eutr.* 1:303. ("humani qualis simulator simius oris")
[51] Long, p. 131.

Claudian then tries another tack, retroactively reading privilege onto Eutropius' life. (How else would he have become consul, if not for some strokes of luck?) For a slave, he says, being unwanted was a boon insofar as it conferred a little personal freedom, and being castrated brought him into the palace and thus benefitted him politically.

"It would have been better had he remained a man," Claudian complains; "had he had his full manly vigour he would still have been a slave."[52] In other words, an enslaved man would never have reached such a high political office that was given only to free men. It is only because of the privilege accorded to eunuchs (despite this one's slave status) that the unthinkable—a eunuch consul—came to pass.

After Eutropius was exiled, Claudian issued a second installment of the poem. It begins with similar invective and then delivers a complex mythic allegory. Eutropius is compared to an infection that requires the amputation of a limb, but removing him as consul, Claudian warns, may prove an insufficient measure. Eunuchs were feared to have "relentlessly malign backstairs influence," in Long's words, and the poem shows the common prejudice that "eunuchs' alien form takes them out of the 'community of human kind,' let alone out of the realm where political decisions should be made."[53]

In Claudian's imaginative work, two war deities, Bellona and Mars, conspire to instigate a military rebellion against Eutropius. Long notes that the attribution of the uprising to "demonic inspiration [is]

---

[52] *Eutr.* 1:56-57. ("profuerat mansisse virum; felicior extat/opprobrio; serviret adhuc, si fortior esset.")
[53] Long, p. 104.

very much in an epic model"[54] and that the poem accuses Eutropius of being unable to manage a revolt for which he bears some responsibility.[55] Eutropius' response to the military attack is compared to that of an ostrich burying its head in the sand.[56] In this tale, he is abandoned by the gods even at sea, as Long notes: "No dolphin will save him. And so may all eunuchs be warned."[57]

Long suspects that Claudian wrote these "two dazzlingly nasty books"[58] mainly because he feared Eutropius' political influence in the Eastern Roman empire. (Claudian sided with Western interests.) After all, she said, "people tend to hate most things they perceive as threatening them."[59] But, she says, perhaps Claudian also simply enjoyed writing the caricature.[60]

That's just the problem: villainous stereotypes are so appealing and yet so injurious. This somewhat fictional poem was used for real political purposes against a real person. It was, as Jacqueline Long put it in the subtitle of her book, "slander."

That's important to understand not just for the sake of a guy who died sixteen hundred years ago, one so long dead that a person today might expect to be able

---

[54] Long, p. 104.
[55] Long, p. 131.
[56] *Eutr.* 2.310-316. ("vasta velut Libyae venantum vocibus ales/cum premitur calidas cursu transmittit harenas/inque modum veli sinuatis flamine pennis/pulverulenta volat; si iam vestigia retro/clara sonent, oblita fugae stat lumine clause/(ridendum!) revoluta caput creditque latere,/quem non ipsa videt.")
[57] Long, p. 39.
[58] Long, p. 3.
[59] Long, p. xi.
[60] Long, p. x.

to enjoy his caricature from a safe distance and happily rhyme his name with the modern English "felonious" and "odious" without offending anyone. It's not just about *him,* whoever he really was. It's about the currency that such stereotypes of sexual and gender deviance still have today. That makes it about us—about how we treat people, or how we are treated, for being eunuchs or for being eunuch-like; about how we make up stories; about how we perceive and invent villains.

General Narses in *Count Belisarius*

Less than a century after Eutropius died, Narses was born into a noble family in Persian Armenia and wound up as a eunuch serving Emperor Justinian I in Constantinople. In this capacity, Narses was to become one of the most famous and successful eunuchs in history. He was given command of thousands of soldiers in the Byzantine army, and he retired from service at an advanced age and died in 573 CE. Usually he is spoken of with admiration. Nonetheless, the English classicist Robert Graves, writing his 1938 novel *Count Belisarius,* managed to paint an unappealing portrait of Narses.

The novel is narrated by a domestic servant named Eugenius who takes a neutral, expository tone throughout. Eugenius happens to be a eunuch himself, although there is no apparent reason why the novelist made this choice, as the narrator's gender is barely ever made noticeable or relevant. (In one instance, he acknowledges that he has "well-trimmed nails" and "plump shoulders"[61] unaccustomed to manual labor; in

---

[61] Graves, p. 373.

another, he congratulates himself on being "a eunuch house-slave playing the hero!"[62] when he kills a man in combat.) Eugenius explains that many boys are castrated to render them ineligible ever to take the throne, which makes them safer to have around the emperor and triples their price on the domestic slave market. He claims that they tend to be miserable, as they imagine they are missing out on manhood, and that "their pettiness in routine matters—I do not deny the pettiness—is a strong conservative force."[63]

Eugenius describes his fellow eunuch Narses as "a dwarfish and repulsively ugly" court chamberlain,[64] "big-buttocked…[with] a squint and a twisted lip."[65] One woman gives Narses the back-handed compliment that he displays "none of the usual traits of a eunuch—luxury, sentimentality, amorousness, and argumentative religiosity."[66] If he had a manly upbringing while still a boy in his homeland, his years spent spinning with women in Constantinople have caused him to forget it. When he gives orders to guards, he exhibits "a very good imitation of a military voice"[67]—not an actual voice, the reader might notice, but merely an imitation of a voice—and others are amused to see him "strutting about in the latest fashion of plate-armour…and high ostrich-plumed helmet and brocaded purple cloak, trailing a full-sized sword which was continually catching between his legs and tripping

---

[62] Graves, p. 252.
[63] Graves, p. 125.
[64] Graves, p. 124.
[65] Graves, p. 278.
[66] Graves, p. 125.
[67] Graves, p. 125.

him up."[68]

When, after Justinian's death, the new Empress Sophia orders him to retire from his command and return to spinning, he gives his legendary retort: "I will spin Her Resplendency such a thread as she shall not unravel all her life."[69] Narses has the idea, at least in this novel, to work both sides of the fence: he advises the king of the Lombards that it is an opportune moment to attack the new emperor Justin, and then he asks Justin for the privilege of leading the fight against the Lombards. Nothing came of his scheme, and he "died of remorse," according to the narrator.[70]

Through Robert Graves' 20th-century eyes, even a successful general such as Narses is made to look silly, incompetent, and scheming, a portrayal that is not incidental to his eunuch status. Graves grants that Narses is better than *most* eunuchs. Ultimately, however, Graves can't manage to show Narses as truly estimable.

Eunuchism Display'd (1718)

Between Claudian's writing at the close of the 4th century and Graves' writing in the early 20th century, there was a continuous tradition of "eunuchophobia" (a fear, hatred, or disgust of eunuchs). Throughout this time, castrated boys and men were taken into service in Constantinople; the city fell from Byzantine to Ottoman control in 1453, but the tradition of eunuchs remained. Boys were still being castrated farther west in Italy through the 18th and early 19th century, not as

---

[68] Graves, p. 279.
[69] Graves, p. 419.
[70] Graves, p. 420.

slaves or servants anymore, but as singers for Christian ceremonies and for the opera stage. Most boys neither wanted nor intended to become eunuchs and could not have fully consented to it. Taking on this gender identity and entering a life of service could convey some privilege but could also constrain autonomy and options. Understood in terms of power dynamics, the very systems that inflicted castration inevitably had an interest in preventing the people they'd injured from becoming too powerful, lest they seek to change or destroy the system. Furthermore, the eunuch gender often seemed mysterious and suspicious to men and women, and thus rumors, superstitions, and prejudice surrounded it.

The Roman Catholic Church was ambivalent about the existence of these singers. Religious authorities did not want to endorse the mutilation of boys, but neither did they want women to perform on stage. The existence of eunuchs, who could sing soprano if castrated before puberty, conveniently solved that "problem." Just because eunuchs were made useful in addressing the Church's anxieties about gender and sexuality did not mean, however, that they would be rewarded with a life free from prejudice against them. They did not entirely *resolve* other people's anxieties about theoretical gender problems, but they were certainly *pulled into* those concerns.

To see prejudices against eunuchs made explicit, it is valuable to look at Robert Samber's 1718 *Eunuchism Display'd*, an English version of Charles Ancillon's 1707 *Traite des Eunuques*. It is a long screed against eunuchs and particularly against their right to marry women. Since I do not know if the English translation—commissioned by a London publisher who trafficked in shock value—is faithful to the original French, and since Ancillon originally seemed to want a bit of distance from his own work anyway (having written under the pseudonym D'Ollincan), I am referring to *Eunuchism Display'd* as Samber's book rather than Ancillon's book.

In one place, this book references *In Eutropium,* demonstrating the impact of Claudian's poem. Samber compares Emperor Arcadius' selection of Eutropius as consul to Emperor Caligula's choice of a horse for the same position several centuries earlier. The influence of a millennium or two of "eunuchophobia" is apparent. Samber says that most people "not only utterly despised and hated [castrated men], but…they could not abide so much as to see them."[71] No matter if "eunuch" was once "a Title of Honour"[72]; it had become a grave insult. Anyone, he says, would like to kill or destroy them and "abolish for ever this abominable Practice out of the World; these are imperfect Creatures, in a Word, Monsters," who manifest "the Avarice, Luxury, or Malice of Men."[73] He portrays court eunuchs as dressed-up monkeys who were seen as "no better than Slaves."[74] They should be forbidden to carry weapons, he says, because eunuchs cannot fight, and if any "great men" happened to be eunuchs then they were "a very particular Exception to that Rule."[75] He rules out any possible defense of eunuchs since "the World" already knows that opinion

---

[71] Ancillon, p. 95.
[72] Ancillon, p. 99.
[73] Ancillon, p. 95.
[74] Ancillon, p. 108.
[75] Ancillon, p. 115.

to be wrong.[76]

Given the popularity of modern arguments against same-sex marriage, the book's main argument will sound familiar: Eunuchs should not be allowed to marry. The objective of marriage is biological reproduction. Eunuchs cannot reproduce. Samber says his argument does not apply to people who have passed their childbearing years because, he claims, as long as one's reproductive anatomy is intact, one always retains a stifled "Faculty of Generation" and thus an elderly couple "may be made use of as Instruments to shew God's Power." That is, a fertility miracle might be bestowed upon them. Eunuchs, however, are told by the author that they cannot receive such miracles.[77]

He acknowledges, too, that another purpose of marriage is to allow a couple to care for each other, and thus an elderly couple has reason to marry—but, for some reason, he believes a covenant of care cannot justify a eunuch's marriage.

Eunuchs who marry, he says, are likely motivated, in contrast to normal men, primarily by the desire to access their wives' money. Thus they "are Cheats, and as such ought to be punish'd...they are guilty of a notorious Act of Falshood, for they put on the Appearance of Men, when they are not so in Reality."[78]

Even when a eunuch is honest in private to his fiancée, his marriage is a public fiction that "make[s] a Semblance to the World as if they could really perform what is required in that State."[79] The woman will be

---

[76] Ancillon, p. 11.
[77] Ancillon, pp. 228-231.
[78] Ancillon, p. 148.
[79] Ancillon, p. 148.

unhappy with her husband's sexual condition, and she may seek sex with others, making her marriage "a Veil and Cover for her own vicious Practices."[80]

We can easily see that any of these situations could befall anyone: A married man and woman might be more interested in money than in raising children, and they might have sexual affairs with others. The selective use of such claims to target eunuchs is therefore illogical and speculative.

The claims in Samber's book also depend on some incorrect information. For one thing, Samber harbors the belief that a man is not fertile unless he retains both testes. This is biologically incorrect, whether or not Samber should have known it three hundred years ago. For another matter, he misrepresents an important Bible passage, leaving out the "not" when he trumpets that "Eunuchs according to the Prophet Isaiah are only dry Trees."[81] This is manifestly the opposite of what Isaiah says in that passage. ("Let *not* the eunuch say 'I am only a dry tree,'" Isaiah says, emphasizing God's assurance to them of "a name better than sons and daughters...an everlasting name that will not be cut off."[82])

The book is also narrow in its cultural scope. While it impressively catalogues real European eunuch individuals and intersperses the list with diverting European folktales, its review of the Ottoman Empire is sparse, and it entirely omits the customs of imperial China and the consequences of the slave trade in

---

[80] Ancillon, pp. 238-239.
[81] Ancillon, p. 95.
[82] Isaiah 56:3-5

Africa.[83]

In failing (for whatever reason) to reckon with imperial systems and slavery, the book does not provide us with an opportunity to use that angle to question why eunuch *slaves* were forbidden to marry. Is there really something about castrated men that needs to be controlled, or do systems of control simply want to perpetuate themselves? That is to say, is there something inherently "wrong" with eunuchs such that it is reasonable to discriminate against them, or do free men simply fear what would happen to their own slot in the social order if *slaves* were given equal power to marry?

---

[83] George Carter Stent, whose mid-19th century service in the British military sent him to India and China, narrowed his focus in the opposite direction. He wrote: "Curiously enough, with one trifling exception, eunuchs are only to be found in eastern despotic countries, the enlightening influence of Christianity preventing such unnatural proceedings being practised in the countries of those who profess it. This serves to show at least one beneficial result of the spread of Christianity; for while we are free from the baneful practice, it is a vile blot on less fortunate countries…" (George Carter Stent, "Chinese Eunuchs," published 1878 in the Journal of the North China branch of the Royal Asiatic Society. The essay is reprinted in Charles Humana's *Keeper of the Bed: A Study of the Eunuch,* London: Arlington Books, 1973. p. 126.) The omission of Byzantine and Italian castrati singers makes this "an erroneous interpretation," according to Howard Chiang (*After Eunuchs,* chap. 1). Deysy Ordóñez-Arreola suggests that Stent may have meant to refer to Italian and Greek eunuchs under the "trifling exception" category. ("Didactic Victorianism: Chinese Eunuchs and Mormon Polygamy in the Late Nineteenth Century." Columbia University, thesis for Master of Arts in East Asian Languages and Cultures, Fall 2013. https://academiccommons.columbia.edu/download/fedora_co ntent/download/ac:179066/content/OrdonezArreola_Eunuchs. pdf Accessed August 22, 2018.)

Furthermore, the Roman *castrati* were singers, not slaves. What prejudice (of unacknowledged or obscure origin, likely carrying over from habitual ways of treating slaves) was stopping these free individuals from marrying?

One detailed history that can contribute to an answer is Pierre Darmon's *Damning the Innocent: A History of the Persecution of the Impotent in pre-Revolutionary France* (originally *Le Tribunal de l'Impuissance*, 1979). Married men accused of reproductive insufficiency were sometimes dragged into court in 17th-century France. Depending on the result of the inquiry, in some cases their wives were permitted to divorce them, but in other cases their wives were taken into state custody. This was part of the cultural context when Charles Ancillon wrote his *Traite des Eunuques* in 1707. Such laws are offensive to our modern sensibilities, and Darmon exhorts readers to recognize that "to debate impotence in the first place is to trigger off a poisonous chain of logic."[84]

The Church, surely, has its opinion on eunuch marriage, and individuals who ground their perspectives in theology, even today, have no shortage of words on the topic of why religious marriage should be limited to "one man and one woman." Some nonreligious people use the same line. Then and now, they take the opportunity to reassert the privileges and duties of men and women and to squash the legal rights of those who have different genders and sexualities.

Prejudice operates in a circular manner: If the eunuch gender felt threatening or unsettling because of existing stereotypes, one way to politically push down

---

[84] Darmon, p. 228-229.

members of that gender was simply to keep reactivating the stereotypes by reminding people of them. Many agendas that seem to appeal to fair considerations are often constructed with prejudices and inaccuracies as their foundation and scaffolding. Thus, the gender category of eunuch remained firmly entrenched with longstanding associations of prostitution and servitude, even when eunuchs were neither prostitutes nor servants.

Once prejudice is articulated and aired, it has a very long shelf life. Awareness of *In Eutropium's* invective from the 4th century enabled a man to reference that material in *Eunuchism Display'd* in the 18th century. A dismissive attitude toward eunuchs even ended up in a 20th-century representation of a 6th-century general who is usually described as impressive. Searching for credible arguments to validate such gender prejudice may not be a valuable exercise at all, ever, and I certainly do not want to try it here. After all, what looks like a logical argument is often just an empty rationalization of some motivation that feels too embarrassing to admit.

CHAPTER TWO
ANXIETIES IN IMPERIAL CHINA

For centuries, imperial China had an extensive eunuch slave system. The emperor typically kept a large harem and also employed eunuchs to run various other parts of government and palace life. The boys and men who were castrated were typically Chinese, not captives from other lands.

Officially, Chinese eunuchs remained slaves, but they gained power in stages. The Han dynasty two thousand years ago, the Tang Dynasty over one thousand years ago, and the Ming dynasty about five hundred years ago gave rise to what historians have called the First, Second, and Third Epochs of the Rise of Eunuchs.[85]

One of the earliest stories of an infamous eunuch is that of Zhao Gao in the 3rd century BCE. After being spared from a death sentence, he became brutal, causing the deaths of other officials and exterminating

---

[85] Chiang, chap. 1.

their families, and even planning a successful coup against the emperor. Prior to the coup, in one famously Orwellian loyalty test, Zhao brought a deer before the emperor, announced that it was a horse, and persuaded some people who were present to take his side in this debate. Those who did not take Zhao's side in "calling a deer a horse" were later executed.

The emperors of the Ming dynasty, which lasted from the 14th to the 17th century, leveraged the eunuchs to offset potential conspiracies in the military and the civil service. There were enough eunuchs—tens of thousands, in this era—that they were organized in a hierarchy to manage each other. Outside the eunuch department, their real power alongside men usually did not hinge on their formal position so much as on their political relationships. For them, as for any palace official, a fall from grace could have a hard landing.

Many castrations were inflicted on boys too young to consent, but many adult Chinese men, too, chose castration as a way to escape poverty and enter palace service. Regardless of whether the individual consented and exactly what he wanted to become or what he hoped to gain, the Chinese tradition required all external male genitalia to be removed prior to entering palace service.

The physical procedure or recovery was sometimes supervised by other eunuchs. As Richard Millant wrote in *Les eunuques à travers les âges* in 1908, an older eunuch was "responsible for ensuring that the mutilation was complete." This was "the first time in a Western language source," as Howard Chiang pointed out, in which Chinese eunuchs were assigned some agency in "their social reproduction."[86] Chiang's observation suggests that, while Western literature didn't typically portray eunuchs as participating in castrations of others, this omission may be historically inaccurate.

This detail is important in part because it influences the reader's assumptions of a eunuch's complicity in inflicting similar injuries on others and perpetuating the tradition. Villainy that consists in *creating* monsters or *becoming* monstrous is a theme frequently dealt with in science fiction and horror, as when a scientist invents, enables, or transforms him- or herself into a dangerous species;[87] this moral question may also hover within literature about eunuchs.

When Eunuchs Fight Back

"Grand eunuchs," the novelist Jeremy Han explains in his 2015 novel *The Prisoners of Fate*, "held as much power as a government minister or a general. Sometimes powerful castrates held dual appointments such as military and civilian. This had led to systemic rivalry between the three institutions—the civil service, the military and the eunuchs." This system was generally functional, but it was seen to backfire, especially in the Ming dynasty as the palace eunuchs grew in number and gained more power as an organized group than others wanted them to have.

The Prisoners of Fate—the second book in a self-published trilogy, sequel to *The Emperor's Prey*—is Han's tale of a rebellion he sets in 1435. It is a long action story, full of combat in which "arterial spray

---

[86] Chiang, chap. 1.
[87] Kaplan, pp. 181, 213.

sullied the wall."[88] Eunuchs order each other around: "You fool! Do you know who I work for? I am the Emperor's personal eunuch! He is afraid of the smell coming from the burnt animals rotting, so the Empress Dowager wants me to personally make sure the Pit of Hair and Blood is cleaned. Do you understand?" (Although this particular order is a false pretense, it sounds credible enough to the character who allows the speaker to pass through.)[89]

In this story, Grand Eunuch Kong Wei initially plots against the boy emperor, while the empress has her own ideas about appointing a regent who will have political independence from the eunuchs. The primary fear is of political violence, but, adding complexity to the story's backdrop, many people are also anxious about demons who assume human form and are reportedly slaughtering palace officials.

Smiling "as coldly as a reptile," with the private awareness that some goals require "violence and hardheartedness," Kong asks one young eunuch to spy on the empress,[90] and his unfortunate pawn only later realizes that he is not meant to escape alive from this assignment.[91] One of Kong's most telling lines is: "I know it is difficult to betray your friends, but sometimes this is the only way to great things."[92] Kong retains another young eunuch—"a slender, gentle-featured hermaphrodite killer [who] no longer thought of himself as male or female"—as an assassin after

---

[88] Han, chap. 12.
[89] Han, chap. 80.
[90] Han, chap. 3.
[91] Han, chap. 51.
[92] Han, chap. 72.

witnessing his use of a live cobra as a lethal weapon.[93] This assassin is always channeling anger about his childhood rape by his stepfather,[94] and eventually he chooses to die by his own cobra rather than surrender.[95]

Kong thinks to himself: "I am a slave, a highly prized animal in a gilded cage." He is aware of the likelihood that he, like other Grand Eunuchs before him, will one day be scapegoated to appease someone. He sees no way to escape this fate, reflecting that "eunuchs were the most dedicated simply because they had nowhere else to go."[96]

The palace, aware of threats against the emperor, attributes them to the eunuch officials in general, and also fears that the eunuchs are plotting against the internal surveillance agency known as the Eastern Depot (*Dongchang*). Ji Gang, commander of the Eastern Depot, believes the eunuch officials are "like a disease. To fight them, you may have to destroy vital organs in the process." In other words, a revolution will inflict an acceptable amount of collateral damage. The palace sees no "soft option" to handle the problem, and thus many eunuchs are massacred.[97]

Ji Gang becomes paranoid about the eunuchs, fearing that someone has informed them about his secretive attempts to install a regent. He boards a ship under his command, and, as it leaves harbor, he instructs, "Bring all the eunuchs before me." Four individuals are stripped of their clothes, and the three

---

[93] Han, chap. 22.
[94] Han, chap. 78.
[95] Han, chap. 86.
[96] Han, chap. 20.
[97] Han, chap. 13.

who are revealed to be eunuchs are immediately tossed overboard. A man who supports Ji Gang's endeavors overall (he leads the bodyguard of Ji Gang's pick for emperor) nonetheless challenges his decision here: "There are thousands of eunuchs. Is every one of them your enemy?" Ji Gang replies: "I do not know if they are innocent or not, but I cannot take that risk."[98] Later, he comments, "Just because they don't have balls does not mean they can't fight. But what makes them deadly is their utter loyalty to [Grand Eunuch] Kong."[99]

To fight back, Kong proposes the creation of a rival surveillance agency, the Western Depot (*Xichang*), that forms its own eunuch army of "secret police" trained in combat and sorcery.[100] After much bloodshed, Kong is sentenced to death by being ripped apart by horses.[101]

As a matter of historical fact, the Eastern Depot was founded in 1420 and the Western Depot was not founded until 1477 (years after the setting of this story[102]). The Western Depot was indeed founded to hunt witches in the harem—particularly to trap Li Zilong, believed to be a crossdressing sorcerer[103] and executed that same year[104]—and it had a rivalry with

---

[98] Han, chap. 16.
[99] Han, chap. 82.
[100] Han, chap. 54.
[101] Han, chap. 89.
[102] At the end of Han's novel, he acknowledges in his "Historical Notes to the Story" that he placed the Western Depot earlier for dramatic purposes.
[103] Shih-shan Henry Tsai. *The Eunuchs in the Ming Dynasty*. State University of New York Press, 1996. p. 115.
[104] "Cultural Legitimacy: A Rumor of a Ghost and its Circulation in Late Imperial China." Xie Yang, Chinese Academy of Social

the older Eastern Depot. The Ming dynasty prevailed, of course, over the eunuch power expressed through the Western Depot. What is notable here for understanding fear of eunuch villains is that, even when they were not individually villainous, they were seen to have power in numbers.

An Infamous Eunuch

One historical eunuch who was considered individually villainous was Liu Jin. He was the corrupt leader of a powerful eunuch group known as the Eight Tigers, said to have been responsible for the arrests of a thousand officials, and he was executed in 1510. His self-castration is reenacted in Wengshan Zhudi's 1891 novel *White Peony (Baimudan)* in which he is shown consuming his own newly severed penis as a remedy to stop the bleeding from his torso.[105] He Mengmei's 1842 novel *The Zhengde Emperor Gallivants in the South (Zhengde you Jiangnan)*—which one scholar described as "scapegoating vilification"—shows Liu, later in his life, consuming the flesh of a young boy, as well as donkey and dog genitals, in a magical, cannibalistic attempt to regrow his own genitals.[106]

The most infamous eunuch, though, was Wei Zhongxian. "The bloody reign of terror during the

---

Sciences. Printed in the conference publication for "Manipulating the Media: News and 'Fake News' in China since Early Modern Times." 7–8 June 2018. p. 62.
http://ccs.ncl.edu.tw/files/%E6%9C%83%E8%AD%B0%E8%AB%96%E6%96%871.pdf Accessed 15 September 2018. This unpublished paper of Dr. Xie is cited with his kind permission.
[105] Keith McMahon, "The Potent Eunuch: The Story of Wei Zhongxian" p. 13.
[106] McMahon, p. 17. McMahon cites He, *Zhengde*, 5.191.

two-year span of 1625 to 1626 signaled Wei Zhongxian's absolute control of the court," H. Laura Wu tells us in "Corpses on Display: Representations of Torture and Pain in the Wei Zhongxian Novels." Originally an illiterate husband and father beset by gambling debts, Wei chose castration and entered imperial service as a menial employee in 1589. Gradually, he eliminated his rivals and gained great power. He enjoyed an intimate friendship with the wet nurse of the young, weak Emperor Tianqi, came to control the Eastern Depot, and rewarded eunuchs loyal to him with important posts. He took to building temples in his own honor, a presumption that would have seemed improper even if an emperor had done it and that generally shocked the populace.

In 1625, Wei's eunuch clique, known as Yandang, brought bribery and corruption charges against their critics. Six prominent critics of the eunuchs, known as the Donglin faction, were tortured into confession. One living prisoner's face was burned beyond recognition; another had pieces of flesh rotting from his body. All of them expired in the fourth, fifth, or sixth week of their ordeal. Wei's abuse of power in this incident was well publicized, and there was communal anger over the matter. The son of one of the Donglin men "wrote in his own blood the account detailing the pain his late father had suffered."[107]

In 1627, the emperor died at age twenty-one. Wei and his associates hatched several failed plots to determine the heir apparent, including passing off Wei's infant relative as the future ruler. At this point, Wei was forced to hang himself. Posthumously, by

---

[107] Wu, p. 47.

decree, his body was sliced and his head displayed publicly. His allies met similarly bad ends.

Stories of Wei's villainy were reflected in contemporary fiction that emerged shortly after his death. The public celebrated Wei's demise by enjoying a series of four short novels exposing his crimes, known collectively as *Wei Zhongxian xilie xiaoshuo*. Three were written within a year of his death, and the fourth was written about sixteen years later. H. Laura Wu identifies these novels in her article "Corpses on Display." Unfortunately, these novels are not readily available in English translation, and I have not read them, but Wu provides a useful, insightful interpretation of all four books, and I credit her work for organizing the following insights.

Regarding the mundane cause of the incident, the novelists primarily blame Wei's cronies for siding with the eunuch to further their own selfish, destructive political ends. As for the incident's meaning, the eunuch clique is seen to have illegitimately gained power, so it is considered appropriate for their henchmen ultimately to suffer their own violent punishment. And as for the incident's aesthetics of the grotesque, Wu says, all of the novelists show the men's first interrogation, although their graphic account of that torture is "more reserved...than some of the sources they rely on for narrative material."[108] These books also try to give psychological or existential interpretations of the torture of the Donglin men (and of violence in general).

The first novel in this series was *Dreams of Yin and Yang to Awake the World (Jingshi yinyang meng)*. It was

---

[108] Wu, p. 47.

written by Chang'an daoren Guoqing who places himself in the story, imagining himself as Wei's personal acquaintance who is positioned to narrate Wei's more private feelings. In assessing the conflict between the eunuch clique and its six torture victims, this novel appeals to "a *zhong-jian* dichotomy, or a model of the morally upright versus the deviant," Wu says.[109] The novel includes only a half-page description of the torture involved in the first interrogation of the six men. It has more to say, however, about Wei's downfall.

The author explains that Wei is posthumously sentenced to have his flesh sliced thousands of times. His corpse (though preserved by supernatural agents that desire to facilitate his ongoing punishment) lacks sufficient flesh after two months underground to complete the prescribed punishment. The executioner pounds the bones, removes the head for display, and offers the flesh to wild beasts, who reject it. Though Wei's earthly ordeal is over, his hell is just beginning. He is chained in Hell along with other reviled eunuchs of the Ming dynasty (including Liu Jin), and they are beaten by ghosts with an iron whip. All of Wei's victims appear in Hell to interrogate and sentence him further. He and his associates are to be reborn as domesticated animals and abused by their masters.

The authors of the second and third novels, by contrast, express pride in the accuracy of their research, according to Wu. Lu Yunlong's *An Account to Condemn the Villainous Wei Zhongxian (Wei Zhongxian xiaoshuo chijianshu)* also blames the Donglin men for their political and moral errors that brought about their own

---

[109] Wu, p. 51.

persecution. Yue Shunri's *Stories of the Courageous Martyrs and Their Efforts to Restore the Great Ming (Huang Ming zhongxing shenglie zhuan)* includes a scene in which Wei orders a prisoner's tongue to be cut and his hands ruined. There is some fictionalization; for example, the six murdered men haunt Wei before his suicide. They taunt him: "Treacherous thief! Now you are in our hands and we will not let you go easily."[110] Robert E. Hegel, in declaring this novel "hardly 'factual,'" points out that it attributes Wei's conception to his mother's rape by a fox spirit, that it claims Wei's penis fell off due to an ulcer he developed after an affair with a prostitute, and that it says a snake-cow god prophesied that he would become a palace eunuch.[111] Of Wei's time in power, Hegel adds, "the text is frequently punctuated by reports of popular protests and natural disasters: the stability of the cosmos is quite literally breaking down." The novelist emphasizes these real-life occurrences "for didactic effect"[112] and ends by showing the emperor regaining his rightful place.[113]

The fourth novel, *Casual Talks about the Taowu Beast (Taowu xianping)*, written anonymously, is dated closer to the end of the Ming dynasty in 1644. Like the first novel in this series, it presents an obviously fictional narrative, and it borrows anecdotes from other sources. Wei is said to be a reincarnated snake.[114] In

---

[110] Wu, p. 50, cites *Shenglie zhuan*, p. 360 in the undated *Guben xiaoshuo jicheng i*.

[111] "Conclusions: Judgments on the Ends of Times." Robert E. Hegel. David Der-wei Wang and Shang Wei, eds. *Dynastic Crisis and Cultural Innovation: From the Late Ming to the Late Qing and Beyond.* Harvard University Asia Center, 2005. p. 532-533.

[112] Hegel, p. 547.

[113] Hegel, p. 533.

[114] Hegel, p. 535.

one of these stories, Wei, not yet a eunuch, manages to benefit illegally from a manslaughter case but is tricked out of the money. Later, overall blame for the torture of the Donglin men is placed on Wei's eunuch clique. This novel expresses a different karmic understanding from the other novels; here, Wu explains, gods or spirits are believed to endorse violence as a way to right wrongs.

The more fictional novels—*Dreams of Yin and Yang to Awake the World* and *Casual Talks about the Taowu Beast*—relish their portrayals of Wei's desperation before he enters palace service. Fiction, Keith McMahon notes in his article "The Potent Eunuch: The Story of Wei Zhongxian," is appreciated for its prerogative to attempt to represent someone's private thoughts. Wei is shown to castrate himself in part to resolve ulcers. While the skin condition is painful enough to lead him to such a drastic remedy and while the remedy is also physically painful, *Dreams of Yin and Yang* says that Wei is too villainous—"a treacherous and evil person, and crude and fearless"[115]—to feel disturbed by his situation. McMahon comments on these representations: "He is like a mock hero passing through mythic ordeals before achieving success."[116]

After Wei's death, a late Ming dynasty novel, *Tales of the True Way (Chanzhen houshi)* by Fang Ruhao, describes a eunuch who "sucks the brains of 490 boys. He takes a gold pipette, heats it up," as McMahon paraphrases it, "and plunges it into the skull of plump young boys." Superficially, this eunuch is pursuing the fountain of youth, but the story represents "evil

---

[115] McMahon. p. 14. Citing: Chang'an daoren, *Jingshi yinyang meng*, 7.35–36.
[116] McMahon. p. 12.

elements eating away at a society that only a high mythic hero could save."[117] Generally, novels in this time period preferred to describe political corruption and brutality as originating in evil personalities, or, as Hegel put it, as being "the product of bad men in powerful places, not of weakness in the imperial system."[118]

The mid-17th century Qing dynasty writer Song Qifeng, active a quarter-century after Wei's death, accused Wei of being incompletely castrated and of having poisoned an emperor with an aphrodisiac.[119] The Chinese anxiety over incomplete castration dated back two millennia to the 3rd century BCE in which a man named Lao Ai was intimately involved with the queen while disguised as a eunuch.[120] Accusing a eunuch of being incompletely castrated was a shorthand way of identifying him as a villain. It was a way of showing him as corrupt and deceptive down to every last inch of flesh.

During Wei's time, as many as 100,000 eunuchs were employed by the government throughout the country, but the Ming dynasty was drawing to a close, and, after Wei's infamy, the number and influence of Chinese eunuchs was greatly reduced. As the early Qing dynasty moved away from the institution of eunuchs, voluntary castration was made punishable by death. This rule was relaxed in the late 18th century and voluntary eunuchs were once again accepted into palace service.

The series of novels that pilloried Wei Zhongxian

---

[117] McMahon. p. 17.
[118] Hegel, p. 535.
[119] McMahon cites *Baishuo*, 3.59, 61.
[120] McMahon, p. 16. Citing Sima Qian, *Shiji*, 85.2505-14.

are examples of how literature can be used to remember crimes, reinforce rumors, and develop assumptions that may be inaccurately applied to an entire group of people.

A Farce of Beheadings

The French novelist Charles Henri Jules Marie Pettit (1875–1948), who had spent time in China, published his farcical novel *Le Fils du Grand Eunuque* in 1920. It was translated as *The Son of the Grand Eunuch* in 1927. (I have, regrettably, been unable to identify the translator.) The powerful character whose commands incite all the action is His Excellency the Grand Eunuch, Li Pi Siao.

He was, Pettit writes, "the most deserving and the most estimable of Grand Eunuchs that anyone could desire. He was moreover of a fine intelligence, crafty of spirit and vengeful of heart."[121] In this description, his vengefulness ranks almost as an afterthought. For this reason, but also because this tale is a comedy, Li Pi Siao is a muted villain. He is not much of a schemer, but he expects that people submit to his orders. If a man is to be castrated, he believes, he should accept his destiny and always keep smiling. Anyone who issues mere words of dissent risks exile or beheading on the order of Li Pi Siao.

Pettit's footnote suggests that the real-life eunuch An Dehai was the basis for his character Li Pi Siao. An served Empress Dowager Cixi and was executed by Empress Dowager Ci'an, prompting a feud between

---

[121] Pettit, p. 4.

the nobles.[122] An was perhaps the final prominent subject of the stories told about real-life eunuch villains, as the institution of eunuchs drew to a close not long after his death in 1869.[123] His successor as the chief eunuch was Li Lianying, who died in 1911. Li Lianying's character apparently is heavily fictionalized in Pettit's novel (and also in a memoir of questionable accuracy, *Décadence Mandchoue,* by Edmund Backhouse who claimed to have had an extended sexual affair with Li wherein he reported that Li was "only nominally a 'castrato'"[124]).

Chinese palace eunuchs were often depicted as gluttonous and staggeringly obese. Accordingly, Li Pi Siao is "sallow" and "flabby," a fact noted by the Emperor and excused by him on the basis that Buddhist monks, too, tend to gain weight.

More attention is given by Pettit to Li Pi Siao's costume than his weight. Especially coming from a French author, this draws attention to the character's Chinese identity. On the opening pages, he is introduced wearing a yellow robe printed with green dragons and an official square hat made of black satin from which dangles scarlet pompoms. His pigtail is oiled and decorated with a silken tassel, and he carries a fly-whisk, specified as another "official" accessory. His long fingernails are "enclosed in pointed sheaths.

---

[122] Pettit, p. 22. His footnote says: "Li Pi Siao's predecessor was named Ngan Te Hai and was nicknamed Siao Ngan Eul. He was assassinated at Tsentsin in 1864 by order of the Empress of the East, Tsen Ngan. He was the favorite of the Empress of the West, Twen Hi, and had been despatched by her on a mission to buy her gowns. His murder occasioned a lifelong feud between the two Empresses." Pettit has the incorrect date of the execution.
[123] McMahon, p. 18.
[124] Chiang, chap. 1.

A green jade ring worn on the left thumb suggested a great scarab held captive by one of the spiders."[125] Moreover: "His head swayed gracefully upon his heron-like neck and his face, hairless and wrinkled, resembled that of a highly respectable old lady." He spoke in a "shrill and strident" falsetto, his nose was a "little mound," and he wore "enormous tortoiseshell spectacles such as are affected by all self-respecting scholars, but these were always removed, as decreed by court ritual, the moment he found himself in the presence of His Majesty the Holy Man, Son of Heaven."[126] None of this marks Li Pi Siao as evil nor even necessarily as intimidating, but it does distinguish him as an important and memorable figure.

Li Pi Siao wants (for psychological or pragmatic reasons not explored in the text) to maintain a social environment where celibacy is considered normal and acceptable. That is, he seems a little sensitive about his eunuch status and does not want it pointed out, even indirectly, in a negative light. He is accustomed to having his orders on this subject respected. Outside his own pavilion at night, when he hears cats in heat, he notes that the yowling is "unpleasantly evocative of the harmonies of his own name," and he enviously yells back to the male cat that only the Emperor "has license or power to love."[127] At dinner with other eunuchs, he loudly insists that food is better than sex. In response to this conversational topic, a young eunuch, overcome by self-pity, keeps moaning "Women..." so Li Pi Siao, annoyed by his ingratitude and ill humor, banishes him

---

[125] Pettit, p. 3.
[126] Pettit, p. 4.
[127] Pettit, p. 10.

from the palace to work as a rural swineherd.[128]

His villainy in this story lies in his treatment of his son and his son's wife. Li Pi Siao was formerly married, and his eldest son, Li Pi Tchou, is slated to become Grand Eunuch succeeding him. However, Li Pi Tchou is married to his beloved Chti and refuses to accept the position—and the body modification it would entail—so his father angrily sends him away.

The novel then occupies itself in the farce of Li Pi Tchou's misadventures. He is repeatedly beaten by other men who seduce his wife. At the apex of violence, monks announce their plans to roast him alive to make him a saint unless he can find someone else to volunteer to take his place. Li Pi Tchou escapes being roasted alive, but he does have to submit to his fate of being castrated to accept his inherited position of Grand Eunuch, and his father suddenly beheads Chti.[129] From the father's perspective, "It was needful to be revenged upon all those who had profaned the estimable name of Li."[130]

A year after its publication, this story was made into a Rodgers and Hart musical called "Chee-Chee" with its book written by Herbert Fields. A white cast performed it thirty-one times over one month in 1928. The storyline differs significantly from the novel's. Li-Pi Tchou (played by William Williams) and his wife Chee-Chee (Helen Ford) conspire to help him gain the Grand Eunuch position currently occupied by his father (George Hassell) without needing to undergo castration. They have the royal surgeon kidnapped and

---

[128] Pettit, p. 14.
[129] Pettit, p. 130
[130] Pettit, p. 131

they play parlor games during a staged surgery.[131]

The musical was revived briefly in 2002 with a mostly Asian-American cast by an organization called Musicals Tonight. According to that script, the "No. 7: Food Solo" song is devoted to comparing a concubine's body parts to "licorice... peas... Edam cheese... hominy... wine... roast beef... oranges... eel... lamb... and pig's feet." Upon Li Pi Siao's entrance at the beginning of the play, the eunuchs exclaim: "The most majestic of domestic officials/The Great G.E., we fear his mighty initials!"

The script is not historically educational. In this comedic depiction, the Grand Eunuch is still a bit villainous, but not really scary. Not only are the individual characters mocked, but the joke carries over to mock the idea of fearing powerful eunuchs. Insofar as the scenes cannot be taken seriously, they may neither significantly contribute to nor challenge gender stereotypes.

In the early 20th century, Sun Yat-sen introduced a new political system. The last emperor Puyi was allowed to live in peace. In 1923 (three years after the original French publication of Pettit's novel), while Puyi was taking inventory of his treasure at Jianfu Palace in the Forbidden City to prevent theft, a large fire caused great destruction. Suspecting arson, Puyi interrogated the eunuchs and learned that some of them had been stealing the treasure. He then ejected all the eunuchs from the palace.

Thus did the eunuch system, punctuated by one final scapegoating of the eunuchs, fade into history. The subject of how related Chinese ideas about gender

---

[131] Thomas S. Hischak's *The Rodgers and Hammerstein Encyclopedia.*

evolved after this point will be revisited in Chapter 6.

Power and Crime

Eunuch influence in imperial China is well remembered today. Its special contribution to eunuch villain stereotypes regards its fear of what can happen when a marginalized group organizes. In no other place were eunuchs employed in such vast numbers with proximity to such enormous power. Though the many recorded crimes implicate only a small percentage of eunuchs—which should remind us that it is political power held by individuals or systems, not gender deviance, that enables cruel offenses—the idea of eunuchs as corrupt and heartless has nevertheless taken root in popular imagination.

CHAPTER THREE
REPRESENTATIONS OF PERSIA

In many people's imaginations, a Persian harem is the most recognizable setting for a eunuch. The large area recognized as Persia changed over time but, to give a sense of it with reference to modern-day states, it included Iran and sometimes extended as far east as India and as far west as Turkey. This chapter presents three fictional eunuchs in stories whose settings loosely correspond to Persian palaces or the idea of them. The first character is Aga Mohamed, who existed in reality as well as in fiction, though he was never a harem servant but was instead castrated for political reasons. The second character is Kazdim, purely fictional, a harem eunuch when the Ottoman Empire fell and subsequently Constantinople's chief of police. The third character is Salmeo, the eunuch in charge of the palace harem, also purely fictional and furthermore living in a setting that is inspired by the old Turkey but is itself a fantasy. All of these characters are thorough villains.

Aga Mohamed

Whatever corruptions might have been exhibited by the Roman consul Eutropius and the Chinese eunuch Wei Zhongxian, Aga Mohamed Khan, Shah of Persia, was far more dangerous. He was fictionalized in James Justinian Morier's 1832 novel *Zohrab, the Hostage*.

Born in 1742, the heir of a prince of the Kajar tribe, Aga Mohamed was deemed a political threat to the dynasty of the ruling Zend tribe. The Persian shah's successor had the five-year-old boy kidnapped, castrated, and held captive in relative comfort at the court of his sister's husband in Shiraz (a city in modern-day Iran). At age thirty-six, upon his captor's death, Aga Mohamed speedily rode hundreds of miles north, seized a caravan, contended with his half-brother, and eventually conquered the Caspian provinces.[132]

Fervently dedicated to the Shi'a branch of Islam, he sought the power due to a Persian shah, which he finally accomplished in 1796 after some twenty years of conflict. The Zend dynasty met with a bloody end, and Aga Mohamed united his own tribe around him and began the Kajar dynasty. He established his new capital in Tehran and fortified a large portion of the city.[133]

"One of his less disgusting habits," writes the British historian Stephen Howarth, "was personally to disembowel any servant who might displease him. With this man, the use of blinding as a punishment—and as a means of making his enemies as impotent as himself—reached a kind of climax." When he defeated the city of Kerman and took the throne, he left no

---

[132] Sykes, pp, 276, 289.
[133] Piggot, pp. 63-68.

doubt about his fierceness. "With his own hands he dug out the eyes of his last rival; and then he ordered that 20,000 pairs of eyes be brought to him from the conquered city."[134] Furthermore, writes John Piggot, he disinterred the remains of the man who had ordered his castration and also of his sister's husband who had kept him captive and reburied them "at the entrance of his palace, so that he might daily have the satisfaction of trampling upon them."[135] As shah, he tortured the old, blind king Rukh Mirzah by pouring molten lead on his head until he gave up the hiding places of his jewels.

It's worth noting that, like Aga Mohamed, Shah Rukh had been mutilated as a small boy in an attempt to eliminate him as a political threat. Shah Rukh had been blinded, not castrated, and, though he managed to gain power anyway, he governed a region smaller than what he might otherwise have inherited. This did not, however, elicit Aga Mohamed's compassion toward him. Thus Howarth finds it "superficial psychology" to attribute Aga Mohamed's cruelty merely to his reaction to having been castrated. He knew his cruelty was politically effective. He was "one of those personalities whom weaker people follow for their own safety."[136]

A year after his coronation, Aga Mohamed was stabbed to death in his own tent in 1797 by two men he had just threatened to execute.

Thirty-five years after his death, the character of Aga Mohamed was resurrected in the three-volume novel *Zohrab, the Hostage*. Its author, James Justinian

---

[134] Stephen Howarth. *The Koh-i-noor Diamond: The History and the Legend*. London: Quartet Books, 1980. pp. 91-92.
[135] Piggot, p. 65.
[136] Howarth, pp. 91-92.

Morier, had served as British ambassador to Persia from 1810 to 1816. Morier explains in his preface that the story is loosely based on real political figures. The real Aga Mohamed "is my prototype," he admits, "and I have placed him in my narrative, as a painter sometimes inserts a dragon or some such monster in the foreground of his landscape."

While Morier never met the villain in the flesh (perhaps fortunately for him), he claims to have spoken to "creditable witnesses" of Aga Mohamed's cruelty. He quotes an injunction to tell reasonable tales: the writer should stick to the way the story is generally known, or else should think of something that hangs together well.[137] His novel inevitably contributed to the way the story became generally known, helping to form this villain's popular legend.

Morier attributes his fictional Aga Mohamed's cruelty to the eunuch's "disgust towards himself" when he contemplated his castrated body. He had a stooped posture, a "blighted and shriveled" physique, sagging skin, and only "a few straggling bristles" to embarrass him "in a country where beards are universally worn." His eyes, however, were bright, "and as they expressed rage, jealousy, or cruelty, made those who were exposed to their fire feel as if they were under the fascination of some blood-seeking monster." No one believed his smiles, as "they were only looked upon as signals of some extraordinary disaster, or as beacons to

---

[137] The line he quoted is: *"Aut famam sequere, aut sibi convenienta finge,"* meaning that one should either follow the well-known story or make up a consistent alternative. This is probably an adaptation of a line I have seen attributed to Horace: *"Aut verum aut sibi conveniente finge."*

warn those in danger to be upon their guard."[138]

At times, in his face, "bereft as it was of its native manliness, all that could be read in it was distrust, envy, and hatred."[139] He was revered by those who perceived him as "so degraded in his person" yet having risen to power "by superiority of intellect."[140]

Even when he was not the center of attention, "his presence produced a sensation of awe that nothing could suppress, which might be likened to the instinct of smaller animals, that feel the neighbourhood of some large and venomous snake, without actually seeing it."[141] Later, when he is counting the huge tray of eyeballs he has ordered, Aga Mohamed's perversity is described as no longer even part of the animal kingdom but rather as "a parasitical plant, which is seen to entwine itself, cover over, and take possession of a large tree..."[142]

In this novel, Aga Mohamed's character starkly contrasts with that of his young, daring prisoner Zohrab. Zohrab approaches him with "head erect and a firm countenance, exhibiting in his person a specimen of manly beauty which strongly contrasted with the degraded form before whom he stood."[143] Zohrab warns Aga Mohamed not to insult his father "who is thy equal, and to whom thou partly owest thy elevation, he, whom compared to thee is as the finest gold to the vilest copper, then I will speak; then I will tell thee, base dog! that I throw back thy odious words

---

[138] Morier, Vol. 1, pp. 10-12.
[139] Morier, Vol. 1, p. 34.
[140] Morier, Vol. 2, pp. 103-104.
[141] Morier, Vol. 1, pp. 174-175.
[142] Morier, Vol. 3, pp. 216-218.
[143] Morier, Vol. 1, p. 111.

to thy face, and that I spit upon thy odious presence. And now do thy worst."[144]

In one scene, Aga Mohamed suddenly, for no comprehensible reason, orders the execution of his chief huntsman.

> His horrid face broke into a demoniacal expression of fury when he saw that there was hesitation in obeying his commands. The ragged skin which fell in furrows down his cheeks began to bloat; the eyes seemed to roll in blood, and the whole frame, from which in general all circulation seemed to fly, wore a purple hue...

He is about to behead the huntsman himself when the executioner finally steps up and does his duty. The sight of the "streams of gore flowing and spouting in all directions" caused Aga Mohamed immediately "to be soothed into quiet," and "his features resumed their wonted dull and leaden expression." He then turns against the executioner for having fulfilled his command:

> "Dog and villain," he exclaimed, "why did you slay my chief huntsman? what demon impelled your officious hand in this deed? well is it for you that there is such a feeling as compassion, and that the Shah can spare as well as he can spill! Go, go! clear up your work, and finish it by wiping your own self from our presence."[145]

This sort of abrupt reversal is typical for him. He is regretful for the loss of his excellent huntsman, but falls short of contrition for having ordered the

---

[144] Morier, Vol. 1, p. 116.
[145] Morier, Vol. 1, pp. 124-126.

execution, blaming the events on the appearance of Zohrab and lamenting his own public embarrassment.

Seated on his throne, dressed in the famous jewels he'd seized, he "became a living illustration of the vanity of life. The jewels in which his person was incased, were contrasted with the ghastliness of his features, whilst those same features seemed to destroy the value of the jewelry."[146]

Zohrab, who incorrectly believes his true love Amima to have been killed and who has been ordered to marry the chief executioner's daughter instead, is, in the third volume of the story, cleverly sprung from jail by his father. Zohrab then has an opportunity to kill Aga Mohamed, but, on principle, he orders the man with the musket to stand down.

> The moment of vengeance elapsed...His own persecutor, the murderer of his Amima, the invader of his country, the announced murderer of himself, his father, mother, and family; the proclaimed shedder of the blood of thousands of innocent people. All this had gone by, and he had refrained from taking vengeance into his own hand. The Mussulman youth felt that such destinies were to be wielded by the hand of an all wise Providence, and not placed at the disposal of a weak and erring mortal such as himself.[147]

This mercy was a mistake, as Zohrab soon sees his father slain, and he himself is beaten and brought to Aga Mohamed. Zohrab asks to be killed immediately so that he can "die without being grateful to thee for any thing" and, more altruistically, so that he may be

---

[146] Morier, Vol. 2, pp. 103-104.
[147] Morier, Vol. 3, pp. 132-133.

the "atoning sacrifice" who prevents further bloodshed. "If thou hast a heart, let my words reach it," Zohrab requests, "and if thou hast a soul, let the fear of a future life and future retribution overtake it." Aga Mohamed calls him a "dog." Zohrab retorts that he is the "father of dogs."[148] Zohrab is sentenced to be paraded backwards on a donkey, spit on, then impaled.[149]

Before this can happen, however, Aga Mohamed is attacked at night by a man who found his own name on a kill list. Aga Mohamed awakens and runs around his bedroom before he is stabbed in the heart. His murderer deposits his severed head in the Grand Vizir's room as a prank.

(Zohrab and his true love Amima, of course, are married. Zohrab, as the hero, has a type of masculinity that his evil eunuch foe does not.)

The unrelenting evil of Aga Mohamed in this novel may have been plausible to contemporary readers who knew that such a person really existed. They may not have felt any moral need for a story that qualified or softened the impact of his crimes, and they may instead have felt satisfied that the story exposed his general awfulness. They may not have needed extended descriptions of his physical sex or gender role, either; if they were familiar with the cultural setting, they knew well enough what a eunuch was. A character who was both evil and castrated could be presented as if those traits were self-evidently linked, although this characterization contributes to, and does not merely draw from, the stereotype. As a result, the novel likely

---

[148] Morier, Vol. 3, p. 213.
[149] Morier, Vol. 3, p. 265.

strengthened the perception that eunuchs tend to perpetrate crimes against humanity and that cruelty is somehow linked to the eunuch gender.

Kazdim

The Western stereotype of Persian eunuchs as cruel had so much currency that, a century after *Zohrab*, there was a bestselling English novel with another such villain. The British writer Dennis Wheatley, whose novels were extremely popular in the early 20th century, wrote a story centered on an unremittingly evil eunuch and the hero he pursued. His novel *The Eunuch of Stamboul*, published in 1935, had a contemporary setting during the presidency of Mustafa Kemal Atatürk (1923–1938) and enjoyed many printings with different cover designs, most of which illustrate the titular eunuch and his many chins. The novel was adapted for film in 1936, released as "The Secret of Stamboul" and also known as "The Spy in White."

The story begins when an English officer, Capt. Swithin Destime, rushes to the aid of an English woman receiving unwanted advances from a strange male at a social dance. He decks Prince Ali of Turkey without realizing who he is. Destime is fired from the military as a diplomatic necessity. He fears that, despite his fluency in Turkish, Arabic, and Greek, he will never get another job, but a private businessman (the father of the woman whose honor he defended) offers him a special covert mission as a spy in Stamboul. The English characters all sail to Constantinople. Rather immediately, the chief of police wises up to him.

The chief of police is also the lone eunuch in this tale. His name is Kazdim Hari Bekar, and he is repeatedly described as fat, ugly, and evil. He lived in

Sultan Abdul Hamid's palace about a decade before the novel's action is set, serving as a harem guard, and had "slain beautiful disobedient odalisques with one of those glittering scimitars"[150]—that is to say, he ran through a few chambermaids with a curved sword. In the palace, he was mentored by 'Twisted Beard' Pasha and also by the Grand Eunuch Djevher Agha (who, just like Kazdim, had "royal proportions and many chins," a feature that, on his last day, resulted in a botched hanging with his head finally stretched "nearly a yard from his shoulders and his great carcass suspended by a rope of neck not thicker than my wrist."[151]).

Kazdim overhears an English-language conversation between Swithin and a Turkish man about a plot to overthrow Mustafa Kemal. He approaches them, warns them that he speaks English, and lets them know he'd like to show them an ancient wall. Although Swithin intuitively feels "intense distrust," he idiotically asks the man if he is a tour guide and, yet more idiotically, he and the Turkish fellow climb into the wall with him.[152] "The repulsive-looking fat man" leads them to an oubliette (a hole through which people are dropped from a great height into a river) and warns them that "such things still might happen to those who are so clever that they make the big mistake."[153]

---

[150] Wheatley, p. 122.
[151] Wheatley, pp. 214-215. I suspect Wheatley got this account of Djevher Agha's hanging from Francis McCullagh's 1910 book *The Fall of Abd-ul-Hamid,* specifically from the 11th chapter, "Cleansing of the City and Dispersal of the Imperial Harem."
[152] Wheatley, p. 88.
[153] Wheatley, pp. 90-91.

That evening, Kazdim presents himself to the same pair again, and the unfortunate Turkish man voluntarily leaves with his assassin. Swithin remains clueless. A woman at the table tells him: "That is the Chief of the Secret Police, Kazdim Hari Bekar, the Eunuch of Stamboul!"[154] She has to explain further: "That man is a monster of sadistic cruelty; 'e 'as never missed an execution an' delights in carrying them out 'imself!"[155]

Swithin comes to speculate smartly that Kazdim did this not to injure the anti-Kemal resistance but rather to protect it from a fellow member he realized had loose lips. Swithin is not smart enough, unfortunately, to avoid entering Kazdim's apartment where armed men await him. It is then Swithin's turn to take a fall. He winds up bound, gagged, semi-conscious, sharing the backseat of a car with Kazdim, being driven to the oubliette.

Kazdim's guards are racially otherized as "huge negroes, naked to the waist, their black skins shiny and glistening, their white eye-balls staring at him with dumb animal curiosity," and as one gives him "a half-imbecile grin" it is apparent "that the man had no tongue—and that they were mutes, old henchmen of the Eunuch's from his Palace days perhaps, the instruments of many hideous crimes under his orders if they could only tell of them."[156] The guards drop Swithin down the hole. Swithin, however, a good swimmer, miraculously survives his attempted execution.

The novelist Wheatley contrasts the "Oriental" and

---

[154] Wheatley, p. 107.
[155] Wheatley, p. 108.
[156] Wheatley, p. 182.

"Western" characters according to his character Swithin's perspective of that distinction:

> Kazdim was so completely Oriental—subtle, shrewd, sadistic, but so certain of himself and showing so little of his emotions that it had seemed a waste of breath to bandy words with him, whereas the [Turkish] Prince was so much more a Western type that Swithin felt almost as if he were up against an exceptionally depraved and brutal specimen of his own kind.[157]

When Swithin brags to the astonished Kazdim that "I have nine lives like a cat," the eunuch thinks of ways to kill him again:

> "give you a drink of strychnine, stick a knife into your liver—shoot you through both lungs—impale you on a stake—hang you by the neck—cut your throat—and, finally, burn your body. Thus will we dispose of the eight lives which you have left, and if I exercise some care, you will, I trust, remain conscious up to the seventh operation—although each would prove fatal in itself after a lapse of time."

Asked by Swithin for alternatives, the eunuch suggests "bowstringing—cutting of the head—flaying—suffocation by pillows—starvation—sewing up in a sack with wild cats—snake-bite—or feeding you to the rats in one of the old cisterns," methods he claims to "have witnessed in my time."[158]

Kazdim has a spy of his own, a young Russian woman who lives in Turkey. After he uses his bare

---

[157] Wheatley, p. 207.
[158] Wheatley, p. 213.

hand to strike her mother dead in front of her, she soon takes revenge on him—to complete the poetry of this novel's extended "fat joke"—by shooting him in the stomach. We don't see him expire and he isn't given any last words, but we are told that he returned fatal gunfire before he died.

There is a lot of information in the novel that helps the reader interpret Kazdim. With the fall of the old Turkish political system around the time of the First World War, Kazdim became the chief of police in the new system. The career trajectory makes sense, as a character explains:

> "Spying's the natural business of a Eunuch. In the big harems there were scores of bonnie lassies wi' only one husband between the lot of them and no natural ootlet fer their passions. At times they'd go fair mad fer the lack of a man, so every harem was riddled wi' plots to smuggle in some lusty young hamal or soldier fer an hour. 'Twas the job of the Eunuchs to match their cunning against that of the women, and the clever ones made a mint o'money at the game. Think of the opportunities fer blackmail in sich a poseetion, mon! When one of these onnotural creatures had nosed out a love affair he'd play the woman like a salmon trout by threatening ta tell the master if she did not find him sil'er enough to still his tongue or, if she were rich, he'd encourage her to play the whore provided he made a guid thing oot of it. But all the time he'd have to go canny as a cat, fer if the woman were caught at her tricks he'd be called on ta answer fer it and if his brother Eunuchs found him out they'd tell on him to curry favour with their boss, so he stood a double

chance of having his fat neck wrung. Can ye tell me a better school than that fer a secret service man?"[159]

That tells us where Kazdim learned the art of trickery, but not why he continues to practice it. We never receive any other information about the formation of Kazdim's character, such as how he came to be castrated or why he is so evil. One of the British characters speculates about Kazdim's "reactionary" political motives for associating with "thugs and grafters": as the new president's political reforms "have probably robbed him of a fortune, he would be among the first to sympathize" with the resistance.[160]

Kazdim is a single-minded spy and assassin and is uniformly charmless in his conversation. He appears to be "[h]uge, sinister, implacable, relentless, as though the passage of time had no meaning for him."[161] When given an opportunity to execute someone, his face is "pasty white and grinning in the torch light, a mask of unutterably cruel enjoyment."[162]

Every time he appears, the reader is reminded of how enormously fat he is. He is tall, is estimated to weigh at least "twenty stone" [280 lbs., or 127 kg],[163] and has a "circumference about two ells [90 in., or 2.3 m] and weight nearly up to that of a Brontosaurus."[164] Sobriquets develop: "the twenty-stone Eunuch,"[165] the

---

[159] Wheatley, p. 56.
[160] Wheatley, p. 116.
[161] Wheatley, p. 133.
[162] Wheatley, p. 182.
[163] Wheatley, p. 87.
[164] Wheatley, p. 164.
[165] Wheatley, p. 172.

"elephantine,"[166] "the Brontosaurus [who] is after her."[167]

> His face was even more unusual than his body, for apparently no neck supported it and it rose straight out of his shoulders like a vast inverted U. The eyes were tiny beads in that great expanse of flesh and almost buried in folds of fat, the cheeks puffed out, yet withered like the skin of a last year's apple, and the mouth was an absurd pink rosebud set above a seemingly endless cascade of chins.[168]

The only things small about him are his feet, "which so miraculously supported that huge body,"[169] his "absurdly small mouth," and his "tiny fluting voice." He has a "vast protruding paunch," and his "enormous sides wobbled and shook as though they were made of jelly."[170] He is more likely to be seen smoking than eating, however. "His great moon-like face broke into a smile of evil enjoyment as he slowly crushed out his cigarette with that air of terrible finality" in one scene.[171] While he smokes, he watches another man "with that unwinking stare by which a snake fascinates a bird."[172] His fatness and his creepiness are terrible to encounter: "as in some awful nightmare, she saw the vast, still form of the Eunuch, overlapping the sides of the armchair, a great pile of cigarette ends making a

---

[166] Wheatley, p. 290.
[167] Wheatley, p. 236.
[168] Wheatley, p. 87.
[169] Wheatley, p. 272.
[170] Wheatley, p. 215.
[171] Wheatley, p. 171.
[172] Wheatley, p. 172.

small mountain in a brass ash tray beside him."[173]

Even the description of his private office contains a fat joke:

> A great satinwood desk, from which a semi-circular portion had been cut to accommodate the stomach of its owner, and a specially made swivel chair of enormous proportions behind it, showed the room to be the Eunuch's special sanctum.[174]

His allegiance to his current superior, Prince Ali, appears revolting ("'To hear is to obey,' O Flower of Holiness,' cringed the Eunuch, bowing again almost to the ground"[175]) in large part because Ali is revolting. When Ali says in front of everyone that he intends to commit a prolonged rape against a captured English woman by making her bathe, dress, and make obeisance to him according to the elaborate harem ritual, Kazdim "smiled with devilish amusement and toyed with the big automatic."[176]

Were one to have the opportunity to rewrite this story, it would certainly be a start to omit the overtly racist comments ("sadistic" character flagged as a "completely Oriental" standard; underdressed "negroes" having "dumb animal curiosity"). One might also consider why "Eunuch" is occasionally capitalized. For characters "like the six-fingered man in *The Princess Bride* and the lion Scar in *The Lion King*," as Matt Kaplan pointed out in *The Science of Monsters*, "their names are their deformity, because the negative

---

[173] Wheatley, p. 271.
[174] Wheatley, p. 290.
[175] Wheatley, p. 218.
[176] Wheatley, p. 295.

essence of the trait represents them so completely."[177] It seems that same identification with a deformity may have happened here for Kazdim; he *is* his castration and therefore is "the Eunuch." The author could have taken a different attitude, however. Another improvement—though this alters the story's entire premise—would be to resolve the question of why a few English people have shown up in Turkey and are interfering in a political coup that they clearly do not understand. This was seen as a weakness in the book even by contemporary perceptions. The London-based publisher and literary critic John Rodker, who in 1937 collaborated with Dennis Wheatley on another project, wrote to another colleague of theirs: "I wonder how you will like the *Eunuch*. Possibly it is too British altogether: too much Union Jack, and yet I can't help thinking it is the stuff for a serial in some popular daily."[178]

Kazdim's style as a murderer, compared to Aga Mohamed's, is less capricious and grotesque, more scheming and efficient. The power he wants is something more subtle and specific than to be absolute ruler of all Persia. It is a challenge for others even to determine what his goal is. He does not waste compassion on those who stand in his way, nor does he reveal interest in anything outside of his goal.

Salmeo

Imagine combining Aga Mohamed's sadism with

---

[177] Kaplan, p. 46.
[178] Handwritten correspondence from John Rodker to Ludmila Savitzky, his French-to-Russian translator, dated Sept. 13 [1937] and retrieved March 6, 2018 at the Harry Ransom Center at the University of Texas, Austin.

Kazdim's precise political machinations. Imagine setting the story in Aga Mohamed's approximate era and giving the character Kazdim's former role as a harem guard. Fiona McIntosh has done something like that, and she created the character of Salmeo.

The setting of the Turkish harem in Istanbul is recreated as it was before the fall of the Ottoman Empire in McIntosh's fantasy trilogy—consisting of the novels *Odalisque, Emissary,* and *Goddess,* published between 2005 and 2007—set in the imaginary land of Percheron. McIntosh was born in England, spent part of her childhood in West Africa, and has lived her adult life in Australia. In her acknowledgments within this trilogy, McIntosh writes that she based her fictional world on the old account of a travel writer though she doesn't say which one.

In reality, the eunuch slaves for the Turkish harem mostly came from Abyssinia and Sudan (the "black eunuchs") and Georgia and Circassia (the "white eunuchs"). By the end of the 16th century, the imperial system racially segregated them. Black eunuchs and white eunuchs were mutilated differently, lived in different quarters, and were assigned different roles. Black eunuchs were mutilated more severely and closely served the sultan and the harem women, while white eunuchs had less impressive jobs involving overseeing male servants.

Segregation is not a feature of McIntosh's fantasy Percherese harem, but race is mentioned. McIntosh emphasizes that her eunuch villain is black, and his personal origin story in a faraway village from where he was snatched by slavers seems an attempt to represent the African slave trade.

Palace eunuchs feature in this trilogy and, in

particular, the head eunuch Salmeo, who is a powerful force throughout all three novels, is a quintessential example of the eunuch villain. Everything he does is pure cruelty and manipulation, attributed to frustration over his castration. On top of that, he is described as physically repulsive.

Like Morier's Aga Mohamed and Wheatley's Kazdim, Salmeo has no redeeming characteristics or moments whatsoever. He fatally poisons two male rulers and is never caught. He disposes of many superfluous male heirs simultaneously by telling the boys to playfully hide in sacks, and then he has them trampled by elephants and burned. He also attempts to poison a female ruler (which goes awry). As the most influential person in the harem, he drives the sequence of events in the story.

He never reveals his origins to anyone except in a brief conversation with his would-be assassin. His backstory, revealed in the third book, is that he is not Percherese by birth. His parents gave him a chieftain's name, Yokabi, and his mother was branded with the name "as proof that she had birthed a new king."[179] From his perspective, he was "denied my birthright"[180] when, at four years old, he watched his mother violently killed by invading slave traders and his father, chained up, cause his own death by deliberately infecting his wounds. Yokabi was taken as a slave. Three years later, he was castrated, at which time he killed his older sister to prevent her from being sold as a sex slave. He loses his birth name and from that point forward is known only by his slave name Salmeo.

---

[179] McIntosh, *Goddess*, p. 284.
[180] McIntosh, *Goddess*, p. 553.

McIntosh gives contradictory information about whether the people who raided his village were Percherese,[181] an unfortunate lapse that prevents us from fully understanding the complexity of Salmeo's anger and ethical indifference toward everyone he meets in Percheron, including the girls and women who, in a sense, are fellow slaves and who in any case he is duty-bound to protect.

As Grand Master Eunuch, Salmeo is "the most powerful man within the palace" apart from the Zar (the Percherese word for the Sultan). He is rich and influential, fearing no one except the Valide, the former Zar's widow and mother of the young Zar. He authorizes all activity, significant and insignificant, within the harem. He buys clothes for the harem women and gives individual permission to female merchants to trade their goods. He orders individual eunuchs to perform physical tasks. He would, if the current Zar were old enough, keep track of when the Zar consorts with any concubine. He is angered when the young Zar asks him to leave the room so he may have a private conversation with a harem girl. The young Zar acknowledges who really has power: "I don't have as much say as everyone seems to think. Salmeo and the Valide are the King and Queen of the harem."[182]

The Valide, who has the marvelous epithet First Wife and Absolute Favorite, dislikes eunuchs and refers to them as "half men."[183] The Valide reminds him that he is not a woman (with comments such as

---

[181] McIntosh, *Goddess,* pp. 173, 553.

[182] McIntosh, *Odalisque,* p. 308.

[183] McIntosh, *Odalisque,* p. 33.

"If you were a woman you'd understand"[184]) and implies to him that he is inferior to both men and women ("Intuition. I've told you before, Salmeo, you may be more woman than man but you cannot think like one of us"[185]). She hates Salmeo but knows she needs him as an ally, as he acutely understands the importance of maintaining "absolute supremacy."

When he is complimented for his intelligence, it is insofar as he uses it in the pursuit of evil. One can't "become Grand Master of the Eunuchs without taking a perverse pleasure in punishment."[186] He keeps his own thoughts and feelings minimally visible. He likes to threaten families, crush spirits, and "put the fear of a thousand angry gods into most people around the palace."[187] To him: "Fear was power."[188]

In this fantasy world, castration is known by three invented names: "Yerzah," or "almost complete," the amputation of the penis; "Xarob," of the testicles; and "Varen," of both.[189] Salmeo experienced Yerzah when he was seven years old. Consequently, he knows "the painful yearning of desire," and only sadism relieves his frustration. He occasionally orders others to be castrated as punishment. From this physical detail, the reader might observe that Salmeo, were he real, should have normal male testosterone levels; it is not low testosterone that would contribute to his obesity, as it might for other eunuchs. Additionally, his mutilation would be atypical for the historical Turkish harem

---

[184] McIntosh, *Emissary*, p. 27.
[185] McIntosh, *Emissary*, p. 370.
[186] McIntosh, *Odalisque*, p. 17.
[187] McIntosh, *Odalisque*, p. 16.
[188] McIntosh, *Odalisque*, p. 169.
[189] McIntosh, *Odalisque*, p. 136.

where the black eunuchs had all their external genitalia removed and the white eunuchs lost only their testicles.

In one instance, while acknowledging the "punishment" that he is overseeing, he adds that a eunuch's life of service is also "privileged."[190] When later we see the "black eunuch boy"[191] who received the treatment—punishment or privilege, according to one's interpretation—he claims to have lost all sexual urges. ("I'm told they got me early enough," he explains.[192]) When Salmeo has another opportunity to punish the same boy, this time by drowning him, the boy begins praying, and Salmeo complains: "Stick that knife of yours into him, executioner. We cannot bear the noise."[193] He demonstrates the villainous trait of lacking sympathy even for people who are very much like himself.

Salmeo's body repulses the other characters. His cheek has a twitching, rope-shaped scar. His face is "normally unreadable,"[194] sometimes "blank,"[195] though sometimes he "smirks,"[196] is "sour-looking,"[197] has "eyes buried deeply amongst the folds of flesh,"[198] or has a "flabby face [that] wobbled with the effort of holding back his own rage,"[199] and his "eyelids narrow a fraction"[200] when he traps someone in one of his

---

[190] McIntosh, *Odalisque*, p. 133.
[191] McIntosh, *Emissary*, p. 311.
[192] McIntosh, *Emissary*, p. 169.
[193] McIntosh, *Emissary*, p. 289.
[194] McIntosh, *Odalisque*, p. 22.
[195] McIntosh, *Odalisque*, p. 406.
[196] McIntosh, *Odalisque*, p. 213.
[197] McIntosh, *Odalisque*, p. 280.
[198] McIntosh, *Emissary*, p. 139.
[199] McIntosh, *Odalisque*, p. 274.
[200] McIntosh, *Emissary*, p. 231.

games. Multiple times his lips are described as either "thick" or "fat."[201]

At least a dozen times we are reminded that he has a gap between his front teeth through which his tongue "flicks,"[202] snakelike, and that he lisps. The simplest morsel of food is described grotesquely: "He bit down on the grape, enjoying the explosion of juice, letting it trickle down his throat...He spat the seeds out."[203]

Even his attempt at hygiene with a signature scent is disgusting: He sweetens his breath with violet perfume, an "unmistakable"[204] and "sickening"[205] fragrance that announces his presence before he is seen and that he "habitually blew over all those he spoke with."[206] He "flounced in confidently,"[207] acknowledges the Zar with a "soft, bouncing bow,"[208] and speaks in an "effeminate, lisping way"[209] that, despite being "gentle,"[210] is used to intimidate. Only when necessary, he "bellowed."[211]

His body is repeatedly described as "bulk."[212] He is a "fat eunuch," a "massive eunuch," an "enormous eunuch" with a "monstrously large form"[213] and, lest

---

[201] McIntosh, *Emissary*, p. 133 (for example).
[202] McIntosh, *Odalisque*, p. 172 (for example).
[203] McIntosh, *Odalisque*, p. 401.
[204] McIntosh, *Emissary*, p. 269.
[205] McIntosh, *Emissary*, p. 205.
[206] McIntosh, *Odalisque*, p. 101.
[207] McIntosh, *Odalisque*, p. 372.
[208] McIntosh, *Odalisque*, p. 372.
[209] McIntosh, *Odalisque*, p. 38.
[210] McIntosh, *Emissary*, p. 229.
[211] McIntosh, *Odalisque*, p. 45.
[212] This word is used seven times in the first book alone. McIntosh, *Odalisque*, pp. 44, 122, 213, 294, 358, 405, 425.
[213] McIntosh, *Emissary*, p. 14.

we think he is large only from the front, we are told that he also has a "massive back." He is a "silent mountain of black flesh,"[214] "huge," "enormous," affecting people with his "sheer size,"[215] "his folds of loose, flabby skin...that had to be lifted away in order for him to be cleaned,"[216] who has "flesh wobbling tremulously."[217]

When the Zar appears, Salmeo, with "much grunting,"[218] is the last to kneel. He has a "huge hand." Sometimes, he is just "the fat black eunuch," "the fat eunuch," or "the fat man."

He seems, surprisingly, to "glide" when he walks.[219] He dresses in "ruffled silks"[220] and has a "chubby, bejeweled finger."[221] He can be found "rocking on the balls of his slippered feet, wearing a smug expression."[222]

His right index fingernail is always kept sharp, as he uses it to perform physical investigations of girls who join the harem; he likes to hurt and humiliate them when he does it, and he keeps it painted red so that they always see it and remember it. A slave maintains his nails for him.

When a girl tells Salmeo that she hates him, he answers with a grin, "Everyone does."[223] On another occasion, a girl tells him: "You can no longer hurt or

---

[214] McIntosh, *Odalisque*, p. 16.
[215] McIntosh, *Odalisque*, p. 17.
[216] McIntosh, *Odalisque*, p. 17.
[217] McIntosh, *Odalisque*, p. 359.
[218] McIntosh, *Odalisque*, p. 21.
[219] McIntosh, *Emissary*, p. 15.
[220] McIntosh, *Emissary*, p. 268.
[221] McIntosh, *Emissary*, p. 134.
[222] McIntosh, *Emissary* p. 357.
[223] McIntosh, *Odalisque*, p. 175.

threaten me, Salmeo. I despise you. But you are nothing, the mere slime that gathers around any powerful person."[224] Of him, a girl says he "is so repulsive to me that I would rather make love to a monkey from your zoo than with him."[225]

Eunuchs in general are not necessarily seen as cowardly or villainous in this fantasy world. A Percherese legend immortalized the heroic story of an incompletely castrated "eunuch" who managed to impregnate one of the Zar's wives and who volunteered to die on her behalf to save her from execution. There is also a red-robed warrior guard called, in plural, the Elim. All are eunuchs, most are castrated as adults, and they are braver than Salmeo, who commands them. One of the Elim, described as a "huge black man,"[226] is given a name within the story (Faraz) and serves as an executioner.

In one case, Salmeo manipulates and frames the head of the Elim and an apprentice torturer, and he forces the senior torturer to lie. Salmeo tells the head of the Elim: "I need a scapegoat and you're the perfect solution. I can't possibly take the blame myself." He promises the unfortunate man that he will care for his children after his death. "It's how much I value what you will do for me. I pledge it. All this will occur if you'll lie for me...and die for me. You are Elim, after all."[227] When the man pauses while delivering his false confession, Salmeo "nudged [him] with his toe" to get him going again.[228] Then, when the senior torturer asks,

---

[224] McIntosh, *Emissary*, p. 339.
[225] McIntosh, *Emissary*, p. 395.
[226] McIntosh, *Emissary*, p. 145.
[227] McIntosh, *Odalisque*, p. 363-364.
[228] McIntosh, *Odalisque*, p. 371.

weeping, what his protégé's fate will be, Salmeo answers, "Who cares?" ("smiling cruelly," of course), and reminds the man that he'll receive a cash reward to "ease your troubled conscience."[229]

On at least one occasion, Salmeo "carefully controlled the fire in his voice,"[230] but, for the most part, he has no appropriate moral reactions. Either he fakes something appropriate, as in "a contrived look of sympathy"[231] or "well-practiced indignation,"[232] or he fails to hide something inappropriate, as in "not-very-well-disguised mirth" or "delight in his Zar's discomfort [that] was all too plain to read on the eunuch's face."[233] When he orders a girl to submit, he says it "lightly, giggling," and "she could see only delight in the eunuch's eyes."[234] He "giggled like one of the young girls in the harem" when informing a girl of her imminent execution,[235] and he introduces her to her executioner "as lightly as if he were introducing a guest for dinner."[236]

Only once does he weep, when it seems that he might be caught for a serious crime that would lead to execution, and "to hear him cry was the most uncomfortable moment" of the young Zar's life.[237] When he can avoid his fate no longer, his assassin asks him to choose how he'd like to die. Salmeo replies, "Swords are so messy. And these are my favorite

---

[229] McIntosh, *Odalisque*, p. 409.
[230] McIntosh, *Emissary*, p. 340.
[231] McIntosh, *Emissary*, p. 140.
[232] McIntosh, *Emissary*, p. 230.
[233] McIntosh, *Emissary*, p. 236.
[234] McIntosh, *Emissary*, p. 134.
[235] McIntosh, *Emissary*, p. 269.
[236] McIntosh, *Emissary*, p. 285.
[237] McIntosh, *Odalisque*, p. 359.

traveling silks. Let's go with the poison."[238] He drinks his own poison, and his assassin decapitates his corpse and brings his head back to the Valide.

The 21st-century readers who pick up this fantasy series may not recognize all the ways in which it is based on the accounts of travel writers to Turkey, and Salmeo may be the first significant eunuch character they've ever encountered. His grotesque characterization nonetheless has deep roots in our collective consciousness. We should realize, from the repeated image of his unusually large body, how hard it is to move or change him. He is a product of many stories that predate him.

Stereotypes

Stereotypes rapidly bubble to the surface in the characters of Aga Mohamed, Kazdim, and Salmeo. First, all of them are described as extremely fat. Prosaically, this may be due to wealthy, sedentary lifestyles and to the disruption of natural male hormones (although, as previously noted, that last point properly should not apply in Salmeo's case). Figuratively, the descriptions of their weight can be used to play off of negative judgments of fatness as grotesque or funny. Second, their racial differences—either in contrast with others who surround them or with the person who narrates their story—are often pointed out. They are also described as sexually frustrated, greedy, power-mad, and scheming, and, above all, they can be cruel and dangerous to anyone around them.

Readers are affected by stereotypes like this. Some

---

[238] McIntosh, *Goddess*, p. 551.

take personal offense. Others absorb the information unconsciously, which carries its own problems. It is important for you as a writer to be aware of characters who fit this mold so that you can decide what you might like to do that is new and different.

CHAPTER FOUR
SEEKERS OF REVENGE

Now that eunuch-employing imperial systems no longer exist, how do writers spin fears about eunuch villains today? Often those fears are expressed through a character who is psychiatrically disturbed.

The Last Castrato is about an Italian singer who, because of the trauma of his castration, becomes a serial killer. I said "is," but I might as well have said "are," as this premise forms the basis of *two* novels, each of which uses that same title. The first was published by John Spencer Hill in 1995 and the second by J. Wolf Sanchez in 2006. (Apart from the shared title and the premise, it is unclear what kind of homage Sanchez meant to pay to Hill.)

Another key piece of the premise shared by both novels is that the eunuch suffers some kind of "split" in his personality (as it was once termed) due to his trauma. The vengeful part of the personality commits the murders. To better understand this, some nuanced background is necessary.

TUCKER LIEBERMAN

Why The Villain Sometimes Manifests as Part of an Ordinary Person

Since ancient times, some conceptions of ethics have referred to right behavior as a balance or moderation of opposing forces. Each of us feels competing motivations at times. Wrong behavior and bad character have often been explained by moral philosophers as the result of evil motivation winning the internal struggle. Everyone, according to this model, is "split"; this becomes a problem only when we do not split in the desired way.

Psychologists have taken a different approach. The diagnosis of "multiple personalities" first appeared in Europe in the 1880s. The idea of a personality split was thus medicalized. In 1886, the Scottish novelist Robert Louis Stevenson published *Strange Case of Dr Jekyll and Mr Hyde,* a wholly fictional story about a respected gentleman who suffers uncontrolled transformations into a murderous *alter ego.*

More recently, it became more commonly accepted to speak of "parts of the self" than of "multiple selves." The division of multiple parts of the self is diagnosed as Dissociative Identity Disorder. The idea is that the "psychobiological subsystems" that make up a personality are normally integrated in complex ways but, for people traumatized early in life, this integration may never occur.[239] The problem is that one part of their personality (including its memories) cannot soothe, inform, or advise other parts, so they have limited insight into their own feelings. They may even be completely unaware of the existence of these other

---

[239] van der Hart, Nijenhuis, and Steele. Preface to *The Haunted Self.*

parts, in which case they have limited insight into the very source of their problem.

Wearied by emotional struggle, sufferers of Dissociative Identity Disorder are "prone to the intrusion of traumatic memories," explain Onno van der Hart, Ellert R. S. Nijenhuis, and Kathy Steele in their 2006 book *The Haunted Self: Structural Dissociation and the Treatment of Chronic Traumatization*. These trauma survivors cannot "accept the painful realities of their lives, and they thus remain stuck in dread, hopelessness, and terror," unable "to regulate overwhelming internal and relational experiences"[240] due to "a lack of cohesion and coordination among these systems that comprise the survivor's personality."[241] Some of these people may frequently feel "numb," while others experience "chronic dysphoria, a sense of urgency about tasks, generalized anxiety, depression, guilt, shame, frustration, irritability, or rage that prevents intimate relational feelings and enjoyment of life."[242]

The late 19th-century Jekyll-and-Hyde assumption about dissociated identity is thus limited and inaccurate. This should not be surprising; it is an entirely made-up monster story. For real people with Dissociative Identity, the "other" part of the self is usually not malevolent and violent like the character of Hyde. It is more likely to resemble a traumatized child. Acquaintances and strangers, if they are aware of the traumatized person's "other part" at all, may incorrectly perceive it as evil simply because it is driven by primal emotions like anger and fear.

---

[240] van der Hart, Nijenhuis, and Steele, p. 1.
[241] van der Hart, Nijenhuis, and Steele, p. 4.
[242] van der Hart, Nijenhuis, and Steele, p. 48.

More recent work has explored how people feel torn, not only for private emotional reasons, but by power systems. The American psychologist Stanley Milgram, working at Yale University in the mid-20th century, "concluded that people become torturers and abusers when they are inside specific dehumanizing social frameworks. Individual monsters are extensions of monstrous institutional systems."[243] Increasingly, today, when most people think of monsters, they may think less of "solitary freaks born of evil parentage or pathological genetics," and more of the products of "abstract alienating systems, social and ideological machines that cannot feel the beating hearts inside them."[244] This includes systems connected to industrialization, totalitarianism, and artificial intelligence.

Informed by these insights, the American psychiatrist Robert Jay Lifton, in his 1986 book *The Nazi Doctors,* found a different use for the idea of a psychic "split" or "doubling." Adults who previously had no difficulty with dissociation may nevertheless compartmentalize their personalities to cope with the stresses of war. This survival technique becomes sinister, Lifton argued, when it enables a person to comply with immoral orders given by totalitarian authorities.[245] Lifton's model connects concerns about

---

[243] Asma, p. 244.
[244] Asma, p. 251.
[245] Robert J. Lifton. *The Nazi Doctors: Medical Killing and the Psychology of Genocide.* 1986. The text of the book is hosted by Pratique de l'Histoire et Dévoiements Négationnistes, an organization that combats Holocaust denial.
https://phdn.org/archives/holocaust-history.org/lifton/LiftonT419.shtml Accessed Sept. 2, 2018.

the integrity of the personality on emotional, moral, and political levels.

On one or more of these counts, many people relate to the feeling or notion of a split within themselves and are wary of its implications. This may explain why the "split" has had great influence in fiction, where it is often used as a plot device to explain why a seemingly ordinary person occasionally behaves in villainous ways. The "split" makes drastic acts understandable for the reader because it takes dark, confusing feelings and brings them into stark relief as an "other self"—something that is a real, everyday experience for a small number of people, but which for most readers is only a literalization of an abstract idea or something that happens extremely infrequently and in passing. Seeing the "split" in fiction also allows most readers to distance themselves from the villainous character insofar as they feel reassured that they do not have that particular psychological affliction and thus do not share the villain's motivations or limitations.

Hill's Novel

In John Spencer Hill's version of *The Last Castrato*, the trouble starts when five men form a secret society called the "*Camerati dell'arte*" (modeled after the original Florentine Camerata association of the arts and humanities), dedicating themselves to reviving Renaissance music in 20th-century Italy. They find a boy, Francesco Pistocchi, about ten years old, who already sings beautifully, and they pay his parents to allow them to take the boy to Florence.

One of the perpetrators recalls the boy's parents as "simple folk" who probably thought he was being taken to "a singing coach or something of the sort."

Italy, however, had a recent history (from the mid-16th century through the 19th century) of deliberately preserving the high voices of boys who sang well. Intending to do things in a historically accurate and proper Renaissance manner, they drug the boy with laudanum, give him a warm bath, and perform the castration at midnight in the candlelit chapel of Santa Maria Novella.

> "The idea was to have the scrotum fully distended so that we could find the right tubes. Anyway, after half an hour we took him out [of the bath] and Cafferelli muttered a few words in Latin over him, then we stretched him out on the altar and snipped his vas deferens." He added, as if to justify the act: "It was quite painless and we employed sterile procedures. The lad was never in any danger."[246]

Years later, the victim recalls how the Roman Catholic cardinal (one of the Camerati) crossed his forehead with bathwater and said, "This is a new beginning. From this day I christen you Farinelli, the last and best of the castrati—in the name of the father, the son, and the holy ghost."[247]

Pistocchi never has an opportunity to sing as an adult castrato. Castration, along with kidnapping and unlawful confinement, is a crime in modern Italy,[248] and no music director is willing to be associated with what was done to this boy. "The lad was simply not a marketable commodity," the perpetrator admits.[249]

---

[246] Hill, p. 176.
[247] Hill, pp. 245-246.
[248] Hill, p. 177.
[249] Hill, p. 179.

They had not fully thought through how they were going to get him on stage without being caught for what they had done to him. What they created was a frustrated, angry person, "a monster—a time-bomb fused to blow up in their faces thirty years later."[250]

Because of the trauma of his castration and his anger at his abusers, the boy Pistocchi grows to have two selves, or two parts of himself that act independently. One is Farinelli, the character the Camerati probably meant to create: quiet, genteel, reflective, with "a pleasant face lit by frank, intelligent eyes that seemed to weigh all they met with a slightly bemused detachment and that also seemed to miss nothing" and a "wistful, melancholy" voice.[251]

> It was as if he had come to interpret his mutilation as the symbol of a universal truth of the human condition—as if he'd understood and been able to accept that, in a way, we're all castrati cut off from truth and absolute knowing by the impotence of our relativity. We see parts, never the whole. We know in part, never in whole. And yet, for all our unknowing, we know that our partness is part of a greater wholeness—and we have faith that, one day, we will come face to face with it.[252]

But then, on the other hand, Pistocchi's separate, aggrieved personality has a single-minded focus on revenge. "Debagged and dumped, that's what I was," he tells himself.[253] In this novel, Francesco does Florence as a crazed eunuch on the loose, a serial killer

---

[250] Hill, p. 112.
[251] Hill, p. 37.
[252] Hill, p. 268.
[253] Hill, p. 263.

the police nickname "Lo Squartatore." Somehow, he "had finally snapped. After bottling up the black poison of his hatred for three decades, he must have been crazier than a shithouse rat and then one day boom! all the fuses in his brain had blown at once."[254] This man is

> consumed by a burning and implacable hatred for those who had wronged him. He was also a simple man—in many ways, even a childish man. His emotions were blunt and visceral desires: not much more, in fact, than savage instincts. There were no grey tones in the palette of his emotional life. His response to events was confined to the primal imperatives of white and black—love and hate—and love was a feeling he had not experienced for many, many years. What he understood best was hatred—and in particular the deep psychological satisfaction of revenge. The wonderful reality about revenge, as he knew from experience, was that it worked. Unlike most other solutions, it actually did make you feel better.[255]

All Pistocchi's violence is symbolic. He cuts the vocal chords of the former members of the Camerati. For the man who had actually taken the knife to him, he plans a special punishment of stuffing his genitals down his throat. When approaching this intended final victim, Pistocchi's "eyes burned like coals in their sockets, and a maniacal grin distorted the curve of his jaw into a twisted, demonic parody of joy."[256]

---

[254] Hill, p. 112.
[255] Hill, p. 60.
[256] Hill, p. 205.

> Pistocchi's actions, of course, could hardly be condoned; but it was easy (almost too easy) to sympathize with the desire for revenge that drove him. The men who had castrated and then abandoned him had done so for gain and with an eye only to their own profit. He had been an object to them—a thing—never a human being. They had mutilated and cheated him out of manhood, had inspired his trust and then betrayed it—all without a qualm or a quiver of conscience. Their interest in him, as Strozzi had made plain that day in Arbati's office, was as a marketable commodity. ... He would be caught and held to account for them [his crimes]. But the guilt for his deeds would have to be shared, before the bar of eternal justice, by the five Camerati who three decades earlier had mutilated him into the avenging angel of their own destruction. They had made a monster, a nemesis, and it had returned to destroy them.[257]

Drawing from stereotypes of stealth and monstrosity, he compares himself to a Native American fighter, acknowledging that the idea resembles "fiction":

> He would make the last two hundred yards on foot, moving stealthily—like an Apache. He liked the idea (learned from American westerns) of the feathered underdog, his knife clenched in his teeth, making a surreptitious attack on the well-guarded fort and then melting without a sound, undetected, into the embalming cover of darkness. Only in the cruel light of morning did the stunned and marveling cavalry-troopers find the scalpless corpse of their

---

[257] Hill, p. 211.

> colonel in his blood-soaked bed, where he had died without a peep or whisper. A feral smile curled at the corners of Pistocchi's lips. The image appealed to his quixotic sense of the proper romance of revenge. He liked to have a little fiction woven into the weft of his reality.[258]

The moral of this novel is not ultimately focused on redemption for Pistocchi nor is it focused on eunuchs in general. It pivots from narrating Pistocchi's tragic unraveling to teaching lessons that men and women can take away from the eunuch's more well-adjusted personality. On that latter point, the book's main female character, Cordelia, perceives that some wives act like a "eunuch helpmate, sapless appendage of her mate,"[259] and she feels that she can identify with the eunuch's frustration of being "consumed" so that there is no way out, only "betrayal," "disempowerment," "loss of selfhood."[260] For Cordelia, Farinelli is a kind of poetic inspiration as she moves from feeling like an unappreciated wife to being a free agent in the world.

For Cordelia's new male love interest, too, the balance between gender polarities is of personal interest. He claims to be working on "a poem called Androgyne, about the paradox of masculine and feminine attributes in human personality. I've been wrestling with it for weeks and, to tell the truth, I don't know any more which of us will end up winning—the heroic poet or the poem that's fighting tooth-and-nail not to be born."[261] Cordelia later explains the poem as

---

[258] Hill, p. 202.
[259] Hill, p. 39.
[260] Hill, p. 246.
[261] Hill, p. 194.

dealing with "the reconciliation of male and female characteristics in human personality. His argument is that we all have both—masculine and feminine traits, that is—and that they're balanced, though in different proportions, in each individual. Personality is the subtle tension of the two held in a creative equilibrium and working together in unison."[262]

Such redemption through psychological balance is not available to the actual eunuch, however, who suffers a permanent break in his personality, commits multiple murders, and then slays himself. It is only the normatively gendered characters, the ones whose physical bodies have not been altered, who are allowed the power to interpret gender as gentle reflections on creativity and freedom and to live out this wisdom.

Sanchez's Novel

At the beginning of J. Wolf Sanchez's version of *The Last Castrato*, set in Florence in 1877, the talented multilingual singer Giaochinno Vespucci is in an asylum due to "neurosis and mania,"[263] having killed his fiancée with a dagger. He claims his fraternal twin Vincenzo made him do it.

By this juncture, Italy's employment of eunuch singers in church and theater music, a tradition hundreds of years old, had been mostly discontinued. One of the doctors comments that "our Signor Vespucci is probably the last of his kind. The world has no need of the castrato anymore."[264] The author adds,

---

[262] Hill, p. 215.
[263] Sanchez, p. 13.
[264] Sanchez, p. 16. Had he really existed at this time, he would not have been the last. In reality, Alessandro Moreschi, who is known today by the sobriquet "The Last Castrato," had been first

narrating within the story: "Since the deliberate process of mutilation was illegal (despite the Church's employment of eunuchs in their choirs), all kinds of reasons were used to justify the existence of a particular castrato, such as disease of the testes or accidental injury—being gored by a wild boar was a common reason. It became, sociologically speaking, an inside joke."[265]

We are told in this story that Giaochinno and Vincenzo are born in 1805 as fraternal twins. When they are about ten years old, their parents sell them to a man who promises them better singing opportunities. The Conte Gaspari has them castrated to preserve their voices. Unlike the boy in John Spencer Hill's novel, these boys don't get a warm bath. They are tied up suddenly and roughly. No opium is wasted on them; they are stunned by compression of their jugular veins. Giaochinno witnesses his brother's castration.[266]

After that, Giaochinno and Vincenzo never acknowledge the impact to their physical sex, that is, until 1829 when the sweet, sensitive Giaochinno takes an interest in a woman and Vincenzo becomes cruel to him. Vincenzo says that he knows Giaochinno masturbates, but what will happen when his girlfriend notices his mutilation? "They all laugh about the half

---

soprano at Rome's basilica of St. John Lateran for four years at this point, but this fact is not revealed in the novel.

[265] Sanchez, p. 92.

[266] The details are contradictory. On page 100, he watched the cutting of his brother from the start, not having been forced into unconsciousness yet. On page 16, he wakes up in the middle of his own castration and sees that his brother's has been completed. Right now, it is enough to know that he had trauma around this kind of experience.

man. The man without a prick!"²⁶⁷ Vincenzo says. "They were talking about how small your manhood must be." He calls Giaochinno's girlfriend a "tramp" and taunts him: "She said you were probably a homosexual. Most eunuchs are, you know." ²⁶⁸

One of the boys—it is not immediately made known to the reader which one—takes revenge for their castration. First, their father is stabbed in his own house with his own knife: "The man was beaten to a pulp, his eyes gouged out, his nipples and genitals sliced off."²⁶⁹ Next, the dying Conte Gaspari is suffocated with a pillow. The third murder is a crime of passion, revealing the murderer's identity to the reader: It is Giaochinno. When he hears his brother taunting him about his fiancée, Giaochinno stabs his fiancée repeatedly. He then threatens to kill his brother, too, but another woman disarms him. Giaochinno then "saw Vincenzo wave goodbye."²⁷⁰

An asylum doctor reveals at the end that Giaochinno imagined, hallucinated, or reenacted his brother Vincenzo in some way as a "psychic twin,"²⁷¹ as his brother did not survive his castration years earlier. Giaochinno was devastated by his brother's death, and this early trauma caused the dissociation of his personality. The moral of the story, according to the author, is that the "real illness" is "hoping against hopelessness."²⁷²

---

[267] Sanchez, p. 124.
[268] Sanchez, p. 197.
[269] Sanchez, p. 154.
[270] Sanchez, p. 219.
[271] Sanchez, p. 223.
[272] Sanchez, p. 225.

Trauma and Danger

In both versions of this tale, an adult has a dissociative identity—one part of which functions normally, the other which is primarily motivated by revenge and a need to kill—and this break with reality is caused by the trauma of childhood castration.

Whether the serial killer's twin brother is long dead (as in Sanchez's *The Last Castrato*) or never existed at all (as in Hill's *The Last Castrato*) is not relevant to his murder victims. In real life, however, this family history would be important to a psychologist who was helping him with his trauma. Family history is therefore something that novelists may also want to consider when writing a character with dissociative identity. Whether a brother ever existed and shared an early trauma is not merely incidental to the formation and isolation of "other parts" of the self. Acknowledging this process is one way that a fictional character with a dissociative identity will appear more humanized and less villainized.

There is potential danger posed by someone who is angry and who is minimally aware of, concerned about, or controlling those feelings. People intuitively recognize this risk. Our immediate concern when faced with someone else's violent rage is (or ought to be) escaping the violence. Only from a safe distance may we evaluate the criminal's psychology and determine what kind of responsibility he bears for his actions.

The ancient Stoics, Stephen Asma says in *On Monsters*, believed that suicide was preferable to allowing one's own emotions to sway oneself into criminality. "There was not," therefore, he writes, "a big conceptual or cultural space in the ancient world for 'victim monsters,' people who might be excused from some portion of responsibility or agency." Everyone, even those beset by madness, was believed to have enough free will to retain the option of self-elimination. Reading into this, Asma sees an implication that some of the Stoics deeply "contemplated their fears of external and internal monsters."[273]

It is worth noting that a split may also be an apt metaphor to describe social divisions. This interpretation would move beyond the subjective sense of self and look at how society is structured into dominant and oppressed groups, "haves" and "have-nots." "It is all very well (and sometimes insightful) to delineate the horrors of the 'split self'—the human subject that projects unpalatable aspects of its self onto despised others," writes David McNally in *Monsters of the Market*. "But it is something else again to analyze the horrors of a *split society.*"[274]

These two novels are not explicitly about social divisions (except for the public eunuch identity that resulted from the tradition of castrato singers). It is, however, possible that one could apply that broader interpretation to extend the metaphor.

---

[273] Asma, p. 60.
[274] McNally, pp. 11-12.

CHAPTER FIVE
SOCIOPATH, VAMPIRE, DEMON

> Sometimes a legend that endures for centuries...endures for a reason.
>
> Mal'akh in Dan Brown's *The Lost Symbol*[275]

The eunuchs in the modern tales *The Wasp Factory, Let Me In,* and *The Lost Symbol* live without conscience. For each, the death of conscience can be traced back to his own castration. If they did not become villains *because of* their castration, it was nevertheless for reasons *related to* their castration, and their ethical dissolution occurred approximately at the same time as their physical change. They do not toggle back and forth between psychic parts of themselves, as we saw in the previous chapter; instead, they have permanently scuttled a previous ethical system and settled into a new way of being that enables evil.

Many novels build up to a revelation—or, in more

---

[275] Brown, p. 28.

modern lingo, a "reveal," to noun the verb—of a key fact that explains the conflict or crisis. *The Last Castrato* novels discussed in the previous chapter are an example of this, as they revealed a different part of the main character's personality. The three novels I will discuss in this chapter also have a reveal, but it works differently. They identify the characters as monsters at the outset and are more transparent about their villainous acts. At the same time, they are less transparent about the characters' genders. This makes sense because the gender category of "eunuch" has become less visible in modern times. There is often some mystery that surrounds a person's gender, and castration nowadays seems more of a private, personalizable detail; we don't always expect to know at the beginning of modern stories which characters are eunuchs, nor exactly what it means for them to be eunuchs.

Accordingly, in *The Wasp Factory,* the meaning of the story hangs on a "gender reveal" at the end. In *Let Me In,* we know that the child is a vampire before we know that he is castrated. His unexplained gender ambiguity seems intended to heighten the sense of creepiness. In *The Lost Symbol,* we find out halfway through the book that the villain is castrated, and then we gradually come to understand what that means to him—he believes it will help him become a demon—even if it cannot mean the same thing to anyone else.

A Child Sociopath

The Wasp Factory was published by the Scottish author Iain Banks in 1984. It was controversial for its graphic, unremitting depictions of animal and child abuse.

Frank Cauldhame, the teenage narrator, reveals at

the beginning of the book that, as a child, he killed a playmate, a younger brother, and a cousin in separate incidents. He was born in 1964 and the third murder occurred in 1973. The manners of their deaths are revealed over the course of the novel. In no case did he use his own hands or a weapon to directly injure his victims. Instead, in all cases, he abused the victims' trust and engineered booby traps in which the victims' actions triggered their own deaths. Each scenario was more elaborate than the last. He narrates with a flat affect, displaying no conscience, and appears to be sociopathic. However, by the time he narrates this story, "nearly seventeen" years old,[276] he says he does not intend to continue in his murderous pursuits. He assures the reader: "It was just a stage I was going through."[277]

He is told that his parents did not register his birth, so he has no legal documentation, "nothing to say I'm alive or have ever existed,"[278] and cannot attend school on the small Scottish island where he has always lived. Publicly, he is supposed to pretend that his father is his uncle and that his brothers are his cousins. He is unclear what his father does for a living. His mother abandoned the family long ago, and he cannot remember her. His ranting, raving older brother (the sibling he didn't kill) lives in a psychiatric hospital because he has burned dogs and sheep. His father keeps an explosive in the basement, and Frank interprets it as "something about a link with the past, or an evil demon we have lurking, a symbol for all our family misdeeds; waiting, perhaps, one day, to surprise

---

[276] Banks, p. 13.
[277] Banks, p. 42.
[278] Banks, p. 14.

us."[279]

The source of his lifelong distress is not fully revealed to him nor to the reader until the end of book. Because of his lack of self-awareness and the contradictory analysis he provides about his own life, Frank may be considered an unreliable narrator.

Frank's father told him that the family dog bit off Frank's male genitals when he was three years old, that the dog was shot, and that the small human body parts were recovered from the dog's stomach and preserved in alcohol. Supposedly this happened on the same day his younger brother was born and their mother abandoned the family. His father only pokes fun at Frank's castration, using phrases in front of him like "better men than you."[280]

Frank refers to the matter as his "little accident"[281] resulting in his "unfortunate disability"[282] and "my loss"[283]; he is "not a full man,"[284] but perhaps "an honorary man" with "uncastrated genes."[285] He complains about being "too plump" due to his lack of testosterone and would prefer to look "dark and menacing" as he feels would befit a murderer. "It isn't fair," he says.[286]

Perceiving a double erasure of his existence—no legal substantiation of his family relationships or his right to attend school, and no physical testimony of his

---

[279] Banks, p. 53.
[280] Banks, p. 56.
[281] Banks, pp. 20, 38, 66, 137.
[282] Banks, p. 17.
[283] Banks, p. 172.
[284] Banks, p. 109.
[285] Banks, p. 118.
[286] Banks, p. 20.

masculine gender—Frank craves power. He is impressed by the power of the sea. "It does things to the world, and so do I; we should both be feared."[287]

Frank has dealt with the stress by digging up the guilty dog's skull, placing a candle in it, and using it as an occult device for what he believes to be spiritual communication with his brother who lives in the hospital.

His only friend is Jamie, identified as a "dwarf,"[288] whom he sometimes physically carries. After committing his first murder, Frank lies to a playmate and says that the "accidental" death appeared to be a divine judgment, adding that he believes in a god who would mete out judgment like that. His father, he says, in contrast to himself, only enjoys "little bits of bogus power"[289] by attempting to keep secrets from him. These details reveal how he perceives life as a power struggle.

While he claims that "there has always been a part of me which has felt guilty about killing" the other children, the "opposition party" of his conscience is "not in power and unlikely to assume it." Later, he imagines a "romantic vision" of his murdered cousin's final hours that does not sound like guilt, and he insists that he has a "genuinely clear conscience." He excuses the murders with the analysis that "children aren't real people" but are "a separate species" of future adults. This is an odd comment coming from a teenager, especially one who was a child himself when he murdered three other children. And, while his first murder was an act of revenge against a child who had

---

[287] Banks, p. 43.
[288] Banks, p. 15.
[289] Banks, p. 16.

burned rabbits, Frank himself burns rabbits, years later, and takes satisfaction in it. For all of these reasons, it is hard to trust what Frank says, but he is the reader's only source of information about his story.

At the end of the book, there is a gender reveal: This child is actually female. His father lied. There never were any male genitals. Frank isn't a eunuch and never was. The truth was always available to him, in his own body, but he never wanted to see it. "I was proud; eunuch but unique; a fierce and noble presence in my lands, a crippled warrior, fallen prince...Now I find I was the fool all along."

As a teenager, having made this self-revelation, Frank acknowledges his past crimes as "appalling" and begins to analyze his motivations for having killed.[290] Maybe, he surmises, he wanted to prevent other children from becoming adults, as he felt he had "no purpose in life or procreation"[291] and regretted that he could not become an adult himself. "There wouldn't be much point to me getting married perhaps," he once commented off-handedly and flatly in a brief digression from the point that he was legally old enough to marry.[292] Later, his insight grows. Believing that he "could never become a man, I—the unmanned—would out-man those around me, and so I became the killer, a small image of the ruthless soldier-hero almost all I've ever seen or read seems to pay strict homage to."[293]

The Wasp Factory is probably not intended as a realistic representation of teenage sociopaths.

---

[290] Banks, p. 182.
[291] Banks, p. 183.
[292] Banks, p. 13.
[293] Banks, p. 183.

(Whether such emotional abuse can produce murderous sociopathy in a child, and whether the revelation of the truth can cure the sociopathy, is a question for psychological professionals.) The novel is instead a symbolic exploration of family secrets and power dynamics.

It is also a play on the stereotype of the eunuch villain. For the young Frank, merely believing in his own eunuch identity (even though he is mistaken about his biological reality) is stressful enough to cause him to become a villain. The cessation of that belief gives him insight into himself and helps him develop more normal ethical boundaries.

Also of note is the family history of mental illness and violence, which could be interpreted as contributing to his murder spree. Any of his family members might have made an interesting narrator. They are all mad. But the novelist chose Frank: the one who believes himself to be a eunuch. Something about Frank's deviant gender makes him a more credible villain, despite his tender age.

A Small Vampire

John Ajvide Lindqvist's 2004 novel *Let Me In* (also known as *Let the Right One In,* and originally published as *Låt den rätte komma in)* is about a vampire who infiltrates a small town in Sweden. Eli is introduced to the reader as a "pretty girl."[294] She moves to town with her apparent father, actually a mortal man under her spell who kills people and bottles their blood to keep the little vampire alive. This man also has a pedophilic interest in the undead creature and thus this novel, like

---

[294] Lindqvist, in the introductory chapter called "The Location."

The Wasp Factory, was also controversial. While appearing to be about twelve, Eli is really over two hundred years old. While appearing to be a girl, Eli is really a castrated boy.

Eli takes a special interest in a bullied boy, Oskar, for reasons that are not immediately clear. She befriends him. She seems to find it important to explain her gender ambiguity to him, a topic she keeps raising: "I'm nothing. Not a child. Not old. Not a boy. Not a girl. Nothing."[295] That she "live[s] on blood" is a detail she saves for later.[296]

Eli eventually disrobes in front of Oskar, revealing a groin containing "nothing. No slit, no penis. Just a smooth surface."[297] She reveals to Oskar that she befriended him because she believes he has the potential to become a killer. Oskar admits that he can envision himself killing, someday, but only "[b]ecause I hate someone….because…they hurt me, because they tease me…"[298] Eli attempts to persuade him that this is the same reason that she needs to kill: survival. Then she kisses him, and, in so doing, transmits a memory. She—*as a boy,* along with several other boys—was captured and restrained by two men, at least one of whom was a vampire. Eli was castrated while conscious. The attacking vampire drank the blood from Eli's wound before biting Eli to feed more. This is how Eli became a eunuch and a vampire. According to her self-reported age, this would have happened in

---

[295] Lindqvist, in the chapter called "Friday: 30 OCTOBER."
[296] Lindqvist, in the chapter called "Saturday: 7 NOVEMBER."
[297] Lindqvist, in the chapter called "Sunday: 8 NOVEMBER [EVENING]."
[298] Lindqvist, in the chapter called "Sunday: 8 NOVEMBER [EVENING]."

the late 18th century. No further reason is given for the castration; perhaps it was simply a convenient way for a vampire to feed.

Oskar, for his part, takes everything mostly in stride. He worries (though his concern seems relatively light) that he has been infected by the kiss and will also become a vampire. Thinking to himself, he "[t]ried to feel if he was in the process of…becoming. Didn't know what that felt like. Eli. How had that actually worked when he…was transformed? To be separated from everything."[299] He notes the irony that "he could somehow accept that she was a vampire, but the idea that she was somehow a boy, that that could be…harder. He knew the word. Fag. Fucking fag. Stuff that Jonny said. To think it was worse to be gay than to be a…"[300]

Eli might have disagreed with him. Being a vampire might be a greater challenge than being gay. As another vampire once told her: "We are so few….most of us kill ourselves….Such a heavy burden, oh my."[301]

The fears expressed about vampires bear some similarities to the fears expressed about any type of person who is considered "other." According to the common versions of the myth, a person contracts the disease of vampirism through an infected bite. When this happens, they are no longer fully human and can never return to what they once were. Normal people may be able to exclude them from their homes as long as they are careful not to deliberately invite them in.

---

[299] Lindqvist, in the chapter called "Sunday: 8 NOVEMBER [EVENING/NIGHT]."
[300] Lindqvist, in the chapter called "Sunday: 8 NOVEMBER."
[301] Lindqvist, in the chapter called "Sunday: 8 NOVEMBER [EVENING/NIGHT]."

Once a vampire is invited in, it can suck a person's energy, either killing them entirely or transforming them into a vampire, too. This idea of "contagion" is common to perceptions of sexual and gender "queerness" in particular. Oskar's character makes this explicit when he reflected that he could more readily acknowledge that his crush ate people than that she was queer and when he was able to express fear that he himself might be turning into a vampire but not that he might be gay.

One of the problems with projecting monstrosity onto others is not just that it slanders or shames them, but that it can incite violence against them. In Nazi Germany, Jews were frequently compared to vampires, and this was used as a pretext to exterminate them. "Hitler, Himmler, Rosenberg, and other early Nazi leaders," explains Eric Kurlander in *Hitler's Monsters: A Supernatural History of the Third Reich,* "refer frequently to monsters—demons, devils, vampires, mummies, and other supernatural tropes—in articulating their views."[302] Himmler once said he believed that peat bogs were haunted by executed homosexuals.[303] The Nazis' sexual experiments (including castration and the administration of sex hormones)[304] upon those labeled sexually deviant may have seemed appropriate to those Nazis who believed they were dealing with *literal monsters*. Thus, in real life, it is important to ask not only why a castrated person might be perceived as a vampire, but why someone perceived as a vampire might wind up castrated. Each question is appropriate to its respective moment.

---

[302] Kurlander, chap. 2.
[303] Kurlander, chap. 8.
[304] Testosterone was first synthesized in 1935.

In *Let Me In,* as the body count rises for the sake of Eli's nourishment, the whole town waits for the solution to the mystery of what they call the Ritual Killer. Within the novel, a person identified as a British reporter explains the fascination with the police department's efforts: "It's a search for the archetypal Monster. This man's appearance, what he's done. He is The Monster, the evil at the heart of all fairy tales. And every time we catch it, we like to pretend it's over for good."[305] In this story, the serial killer, the "archetypal Monster," just happens to take the form of a castrated child: one who can never grow up and can never be defeated as long as he persuades others to maintain him in his villainous, undead, compromised state.

Although a victim of a pedophile, the child is shown as the one in control of the relationship; the boy *literally* preys on the adult, in the end, as vampires tend to do. The blame for the eunuch vampire's situation is implicitly placed on him for being what he is, and also for not, unlike other vampires, choosing instead to kill himself.

A Man Who Aspires to Be a Demon

The action in Dan Brown's 2009 thriller *The Lost Symbol* depends on its castrated villain, Mal'akh, whose hot pursuit of a Masonic secret places time pressure on the heroes to stop him. Mal'akh's story is revealed gradually and in flashbacks. Putting his details in chronological order would result in the following narrative.

---

[305] Lindqvist, in the chapter called "Sunday: 8 NOVEMBER [EVENING]."

PAINTING DRAGONS

Zachary Solomon is born into an extremely wealthy American family. At age eighteen, his father, a significant figure in Masonry, offers him a choice of inheritance: "wealth or wisdom."[306] To his father's chagrin, Zachary chooses the money; he wants nothing to do with the wisdom, even when his father revises the offer to clarify that he can have both.

The teenager soon winds up in a Turkish prison on a cocaine violation. It is his first identity transformation: He is now "Inmate 37." His father, expecting that his son will soon be released anyway with the help of the State Department, flies to Turkey to negotiate an earlier release. The guard wants a bribe. The father has no intention of offering money; he believes his son needs to learn accountability, and buying him out of jail seems a step too far. He flies home without his son.

Zachary overhears his father's refusal to pay the bribe and perceives it as an unforgivable abandonment. It is the grudge that animates his evil machinations for the rest of his life.

Wielding false promises of money, Zachary sweet-talks the guard into letting him out. He fakes his own death, which directly involves the murder of two people at the prison and indirectly leads to his grieving parents' divorce.

His identity transformation places him in a life of leisure in Greece under an assumed name. He focuses on self-beautification, taking "aggressive cycles of steroids intermixed with black-market growth hormones and endless hours of weight lifting" to

---

[306] Brown, p. 301.

become "a perfect male specimen."[307] From this, "his vocal cords had been ravaged, transforming his boyish voice into a permanent whisper."[308] After some years, paradise bores him. He comes to realize he's made a mistake in choosing wealth over wisdom.

In his mid-twenties, pretending to be the man who murdered Zachary in prison, he bursts into a family Christmas gathering and asks for "Zachary's other birthright," the Masonic secret of wisdom.[309] When this is not forthcoming, he fatally shoots his father's mother. She returns fire, scarring him with birdshot. Still without revealing his identity, he taunts his father: "What kind of man leaves his son in a prison when he has the option to get him out! You killed your son! Not me."[310] He escapes the scene.

He begins tattooing himself to hide his scars from the birdshot. Eventually his entire six-foot-three frame is permanently decorated: his feet like a hawk's, his legs and groin like the marble columns of a building, his "massive sex organ" with symbols, his chest with a "double-headed phoenix," his arms with scales, and from shaved head to shoulders with "an intricate tapestry of ancient symbols and sigils." He thinks of himself as "masterpiece," "artifact," "evolving icon."[311] He has to wear foundation makeup to blend into a crowd.

For his new identity transformation, he calls himself Mal'akh, inspired by the name of an angel from Milton's *Paradise Lost*. He also chooses castration.

---

[307] Brown, p. 282.
[308] Brown, p. 561.
[309] Brown, p. 259.
[310] Brown, p. 286.
[311] Brown, p. 14, 336.

Like the mystical eunuch monks of Katharoi, Mal'akh had removed his testicles. He had sacrificed his physical potency for a more worthy one. Gods have no gender. Having shed the human imperfection of gender along with the earthly pull of sexual temptation, Mal'akh had become like Ouranos, Attis, Sporus, and the great castrati magicians of Arthurian legend. Every spiritual metamorphosis is preceded by a physical one. Such was the lesson of all the great gods…from Osiris, to Tammuz, to Jesus, to Shiva, to the Buddha himself.

I must shed the man who clothes me.[312]

* * *

Castration had been less painful than he had imagined....Like the mythological self-castrated Attis, Mal'akh knew that achieving immortality required a clean break with the material world of male and female.

The androgyne is one.

Nowadays, eunuchs were shunned, although the ancients understood the

---

[312] Brown, p. 336. A note regarding the Katharoi monastery: Shaun Tougher in *The Eunuch in Byzantine History and Society* (Abingdon and New York: Routledge, 2008) says that while this monastery was built by Narses (the eunuch discussed in Chapter 1 of *Painting Dragons*), it's unclear that it was intended specifically for eunuch monks. The only evidence "is the name itself, which means 'The Pure'. Thus, it must be considered a doubtful identification."

> inherent power of this transmutational sacrifice.[313]

Dan Brown does not go further, possibly so as not to offend a huge audience that includes many religious Christians, in describing the castration's physical reality nor in explaining its meaning to Mal'akh. We aren't told, for example, whether it is a ritual necessity for a magic spell, whether it is supposed to help him control his mood, or whether he got what he came for. The mystery of exactly how that is supposed to work remains mostly preserved. Perhaps it must be this way; after all, outside the novel, demons do not exist, so it is difficult to explain how they operate.

Mal'akh was evil before he became a eunuch. The "demon reveal" is more important than the "eunuch reveal." Castration was part of his delusional transformation, a symptom of his illness, not—as with the other eunuchs reviewed in this book—the alleged cause of it. Nonetheless, since his move to the dark side causes him to pursue radical body modification, castration remains a frightening feature and a hallmark of his villainy.

Ten years after shooting his grandmother, Mal'akh kidnaps his father, amputates his father's hand, and tattoos his own head with his father's blood. He is also willing to put his father's sister in his crosshairs as soon as he can access her secrets. He kills (or tries to kill) a number of people who stand in his way, some in especially diabolical ways that require forethought and setup. While torturing his family members, he continues to hide his original identity from them. They do not know that he is Zachary Solomon, a man whose

---

[313] Brown, p. 406.

death was faked and whose identity has been transformed.

What Mal'akh really wants is for his father to kill him in a ritual sacrifice that reenacts Abraham's attempted sacrifice of Isaac in the Bible. Mal'akh believes this is the way to "establish his rank in the hierarchy of demons."[314] This is the "demon reveal" that follows the "eunuch reveal."

He is content to be evil:

> *Hate me*, Mal'akh thought. *The greater the emotion, the more potent the energy that will be released when the ritual is completed.*[315]

He sees good and evil as roughly equivalent in the grand scheme of things, perhaps as merely different interpretations of the same events or as forces that push and pull. After all, "the guardian angel who conquered your enemy in battle was perceived by your enemy as a demon destroyer."[316]

> All the ancient texts spoke of good and evil…and of man's need to choose between them. *I made my choice long ago*, he knew, and yet he felt no remorse. *What is evil, if not a natural law?*[317]

As he finally reveals his identity to his father, he asks rhetorically: "What kind of father gives a child the choice between 'wealth or wisdom' and expects him to know how to handle it!"[318] We might expect the grudge to have worn thin by this point. Most people would

---

[314] Brown, p. 558.
[315] Brown, p. 550.
[316] Brown, p. 15.
[317] Brown, p. 362.
[318] Brown, p. 559.

have shrugged it off (along with any grudges related to a brief imprisonment for their own teenage drug violation) after sixteen years. But then, most people haven't castrated themselves to transform into demons.

Apart from murder, which ordinary humans can accomplish, Mal'akh doesn't *do* much that vouches for his demonic nature. It is what he *feels* that makes him a demon. He has unrelenting hate.

"One aspect of the monster concept seems to be the breakdown of intelligibility," Stephen Asma writes in *On Monsters*. "An action or a person or a thing is monstrous when it can't be processed by our rationality, and also when we cannot readily relate to the emotional range involved. We know what it's like to hate, for example, but when we designate a monstrous hate, we are acknowledging that it is off our chart."[319] Mal'akh is meant to be seen as off the chart.

Around the same time as Brown published *The Lost Symbol*, the American thriller writer Dean Koontz published *Lost Souls*. This is the fourth book in Koontz's *Frankenstein* series that monitors the escapades of post-human created beings. In this story, Victor, a mad scientist, endures a new physical incarnation. The old Victor enjoyed raping female clones that he created. The new Victor has bigger goals: achieve absolute power, destroy all humans and post-human clones, see that the universe is empty, assure that the Bible's content shrinks to the first page of Genesis, reject "the value of both power and creation," and then kill himself. In service of this demonic goal, his first act in his new body is to be "neutered" at a

---

[319] Asma, p. 10.

medical clinic so he can avoid the distraction of the sexual "power fantasies" that beset his old self.[320] This rationalization for castration seems thin: What is the plan to destroy the world, if not itself a power fantasy? But because his castration is not mentioned further, it resists analysis. Victor's mysterious body modification in *Lost Souls* and Mal'akh's similar choice in *Lost Symbol*, viewed together, suggest that voluntary castration is simply a thing that demons do.

Other Serial Killers with a Feminine Gender Reveal

When Frank Cauldhame in *The Wasp Factory* realizes that he has always been biologically female, he loses all murderous urges and never kills again. His identity as a castrated boy was never a matter of personal preference or self-actualization; it was the result of being misled by adults about facts of human biology and of his own life story. The eunuch identity was the result of deception, and it produced the behavior of a fictional eunuch villain. Coming to see himself as a girl, then, makes this character whole.

In other stories, by contrast, a serial killer who is biologically male experiences some apparent gender confusion and gives some cues that he may have a feminine identity (whether well-developed or no). In these cases, the feminine identity is tied to the evil that the killer perpetrates. It is portrayed as part of the serial killer's ongoing deceptions and as part of the motive for his crimes.

Mal'akh in *The Lost Symbol* lays claim to sacred androgyny, but it seems he is missing the point. Being

---

[320] Koontz, p. 261.

androgynous is sometimes understood as being neither masculine nor feminine, but Mal'akh hasn't identified anything specific about masculinity that he'd like to leave behind nor has he demonstrated an attempt to do so. Being androgynous can also be interpreted as being *both* masculine *and* feminine—as in the references to a character's poem "Androgyne" in John Spencer Hill's *The Last Castrato* discussed in the previous chapter—but there is nothing apparently feminine about the way Mal'akh muscles through his killing spree, and there is nothing balanced about his personality. Maybe he just likes the sound of the word "androgyny." There would be nothing wrong with that attitude if he were an ordinary person. But, for a full-time seeker of wisdom who aspires to a level of knowledge that will make him a demon god, that level of commitment seems weak. He may be deceiving even himself.

Additionally, two American novels, Robert Bloch's *Psycho* (1959) and Thomas Harris' *The Silence of the Lambs* (1988), famously feature a serial killer with a dissociated personality. In *Psycho,* a man dresses up as his own mother when he kills women. In *The Silence of the Lambs,* a man kills overweight women and skins them to sew a "girl-suit" for himself to wear.[321] These premises leverage the fear of gender deviance and, more specifically, try to prompt us to question our own

---

[321] The detectives are most concerned with stopping his killing spree, not with assessing his gender. Readers have debated whether this character, whose request for sex-reassignment surgery was denied due to his mental illness, is "actually" a transgender woman. This is a hard question to answer not only because of the difficulty of defining someone else's gender but because the person in question is fictional. Answers to the question might lie in fanfiction.

ability to distinguish between someone who merely has an unusual gender presentation and someone who is going to kill us. Maybe the underlying cultural fear is that someone who has ideas about surgically modifying his own body might be on the lookout to carve up others, too. Upon reflection, this fear seems obviously misplaced, since we don't assume that a desire to modify one's own body in more common ways (e.g. tattoos, cosmetic surgery) imply a desire to force a modification on anyone else. And yet, this fear emerges specifically for gender-transgressive body modifications.

"I'll be really happy if I never see another murderer who's revealed to be trans," the transgender actor Harvey Zielinski told a journalist in 2018. "Or a psychopath, or someone with debilitating mental illness" whose transgender identity constitutes "the big twist…I'm pretty done with that narrative. It's pretty obviously problematic."[322]

It is not necessarily bad that a few of these stories were created. They have entertained many people over the years. But it is precisely their wild popularity and their memorability—even today—that suggest these stories tap into ongoing fears of gender-deviant people. That's part of why they were successful. The stereotypes already existed. What we experience when we read these stories is a sign that points to cultural beliefs about gender-deviant people, including beliefs about eunuch villains.

---

[322] "Murderers or mentally ill: The problematic history of transgender characters on screen." Anna Kelsey-Sugg. Australian Broadcasting Corporation (ABC News), 15 August 2018. http://www.abc.net.au/news/2018-08-16/changing-media-representations-of-trans-people/10114402

CHAPTER SIX
MEANINGS IN MODERN EMPIRE

Recognizing that stories about evilly distorted personalities can drive off of transgender identity, too, there is another book we should consider. This is not a story. But it is fiction.

When I was in college two decades ago, I found a copy of Janice Raymond's *The Transsexual Empire: The Making of the She-Male*, a 1979 screed against transgender people. It was reprinted in 1994 with a new introduction that clarifies and intensifies her original message without retracting a word of it.[323] Today, in 2018, not only does she still defend what she wrote, but she even offers the book as a free download. On her website, she complains about misquotations of her book and "defamatory" attacks against herself without

---

[323] In 2033, when this book on eunuch villains is fifteen years old, I hope and expect to find many passages I would like to change. Please ask me at that time how I would like to self-critique my own 15th-anniversary introduction.

acknowledging that anything she said may have hurt someone else, and she continues to deny that "hormones and surgery transform men into women and women into men."[324]

Her critique is directed at transgender women, since (at least as of the 1994 edition that she is still distributing) she believes there are no significant numbers of transgender men. I myself am a transgender man. I don't know how many of me would make me significant to her. When I pick up this book—containing its assessments of my identity, with its simultaneous skepticism of the likelihood of my existence—I feel like a fly on the wall...who can read.

Supported by prominent feminists, the book had a wide audience in its day; there were few books available on "transsexualism"[325] at the time. Naturally I immediately recognized *The Transsexual Empire* as a political affront to me and my kind. Today, I have a better idea of where the assumptions and prejudice come from.

To Raymond, womanness or femaleness is determined by the personal "history" of living "in a female body."[326] She has no problem with breaking gender norms. In fact, she advocates dismantling them. She wants the same behavior to be socially permitted to all, regardless of who happens to be a woman or a

---

[324] "Fictions and Facts about the Transsexual Empire." Janice G. Raymond: Official Author Site.
http://janiceraymond.com/fictions-and-facts-about-the-transsexual-empire Accessed Aug. 4, 2018.
[325] This term is considered outdated.
[326] Janice G. Raymond. *The Transsexual Empire: The Making of the She-Male.* New York and London: Teachers College Press, 1994. (Originally Boston: Beacon Press, 1979). Introduction, p. xx.

man. She emphasizes, however, that someone's gender itself can never change. To her, gender isn't defined by genitals, hormones, nor by an appeal to some mysterious feature of brain/mind. It is only determined by one's history of living in a certain body, and that history is an unchanging fact.

As soon as someone questions or rejects the entire category of "woman" or "man" that has been assigned to them, their gender becomes threatening or displeasing to Raymond. She assumes that a person who abandons one gender category for another does so mainly to reject one set of prescribed behavior and to embrace different norms. She also assumes that the person seeks social acceptance of their gender transition not only to legitimize their personal identity but, more insidiously, to validate the gender stereotypes that explain their motivation for gender transition. (To make a simple example of Raymond's point: A transgender woman may wear a skirt to demonstrate feminine identity, but, in using a skirt to "prove" her femininity or to help others interpret her as a woman, she reinforces the sexist rule that skirts are for women and not for men.) Raymond thinks that transsexualism is an exercise in conformity and that transsexuals operate within the gender binary, being pushed and pulled by its dark forces, without questioning the system. She thinks that "transsexually-constructed" women's gender identity or presentation is an unironic "caricature" of the very feminine ideals that are common objects of feminist critique.

Transition from one gender to another, she claims, is the opposite of taking a brave political stand to abolish the "social constraints" of gender roles. She seems to believe that if people were free to dress, dance, and date as they pleased, then gender would be personally and politically irrelevant and no one would have any qualms about the gender that had been assigned to them.

This argument is made of misconceptions and prejudices, and it is a political attack on transgender people. Raymond forms a catch-22 that double-binds her victim: When transgender women *do* seek political solidarity with other women, she counts that action against them, because, in her view, they do so only to "possess" or "assimilate"[327] other women's power. Any interest in or care for other women they might express is interpreted, by her, as an insidious attempt at seeking validation for themselves.

So, if a transgender woman so much as shows up in a room to support whatever political project Raymond might endorse, the woman would appear to Raymond as acting in bad faith, likely as a counterproductive presence and possibly as an enemy, simply because of the woman's self-determined gender identity. To Raymond, all transgender people are energy vampires. Our motivations can never be pure because our gender is confusing to her. The harder we work at being good people, the more she is distressed by having to look at our faces. When we are good, we are posing as copies of the real thing—real gender, real body, real virtue—possessing and assimilating other people's goodness. When we are not good, we are not merely insufficient or mistaken, but we reflect caricatures of badness; that is, we are *villains*.

This was wrong in 1979, it was wrong in 1994, and it is wrong today in 2018. As a transgender person who

---

[327] Raymond, Introduction, p. xxi.

spent the first half of my life in an assigned female role and the more recent half of my life in an assigned male role, and who has (not unrelated to that fact) spent a good deal of my life in conversation with people whose journeys have been similar to mine, I have acquired a relevant perspective. I can unequivocally say this: Transgender people have feelings *and* cultural analysis *and* political ideals, and, in the ways we experience our lives and act on our beliefs, we are every bit as diverse as people who do not identify as transgender. Undergoing surgery between one's legs (for those who do it) indeed requires a large investment of inward-directed attention for that specific procedure, but it does not render one incapable of outward-directed solidarity in other areas of life. It is only for the brief anesthetic-induced unconsciousness that I would be a thoroughly apolitical creature, and my life is not defined by that hour on the surgeon's table, regardless of how important the result is to me.

Here's how Raymond's book relates to eunuch villain characters. To convince others to be scared of transgender women and to reinforce the impression that they are really men, she conjures up the older concept of eunuchs. Her book's index calls eunuchs the "forerunners" of today's transgender women.[328]

> Eunuchs were men that other more powerful men used to keep their women in place....the word *eunuch* is also related to the word *scheme*. (Eunuchs schemed to

---

[328] The text of her book is not very clear in explaining the connection. She says that castrated men in history are the "antecedents" of modern transgender women's experience even if they are not "strictly speaking...precedents." See Raymond, p. 20.

> obtain political power.)...[they] always attached themselves to women's spaces and, most frequently, were used to supervise women's freedom of movement and to harness women's self-centeredness and self-government.[329]

Today's transgender women, particularly those who identify as "lesbian-feminists," inherit the eunuch's role, she says, in that "their whole presence becomes a 'member' invading women's presence and dividing us once more from each other."[330] A transgender woman may relinquish the external genitalia with which she was born, but it seems that she can never escape its specter, at least in Raymond's mind. Raymond has, in the sentence just quoted, accused transgender women (and eunuchs before them) of being, metaphorically, giant walking penises. She accuses them of being somehow defined by the very part that isn't there anymore, has been disabled or modified or reconceptualized, or is felt by its owner to be irrelevant. This is a schoolyard insult—"their whole presence becomes a 'member,'" stated publicly so that "they" can hear, means *you are a penis*—and it doesn't even make sense.

Will accepting transgender women, she asks, "lead to the containment and control of lesbian-feminists? Will every lesbian-feminist space become a harem?"[331]

Literally? Of course not. Western lesbians and feminists are not living in confinement, and transgender women not guarding the keys to the closet. If Raymond had any reason for suspecting four

---

[329] Raymond, p. 105.
[330] Raymond, p. 104. She cites the idea to Mary Daly.
[331] Raymond, p. 105.

decades ago that this would happen, those harems are lagging in their construction schedule.

Figuratively? Still, no. Transgender people's voices are increasingly heard, but the airing of our opinions does not mean that we have muzzled anyone else's speech. Voicing an argument or winning a debate does not make one an evil harem eunuch. Having reconstructive genital surgery does not increase the likelihood of becoming an evil harem eunuch, either.

What, then, is she trying to say here? I think she is blaming gender oppression on the existence of those who subvert gender in a way that differs from the way in which she likes to subvert gender. I find this blame game counterproductive and inaccurate. It is not the presence of sexually complicated people that causes oppressive systems to arise. After all, oppressive systems tend to hurt the deviants first. We don't want those systems either.

To speak about the historical problem: Since eunuchs were in a position to oppress other eunuchs, women, and men only because they, too, were oppressed, one could easily criticize the whole system that dragged everyone down into deceit and conflict in the struggle for survival. To criticize the system would seem more kind, correct, and fruitful than to criticize a randomly selected handful of individuals caught up in the system. I think Raymond should be persuadable on this, given her asserted interest in moving from private feelings to political consciousness. She does, to be fair to her, express awareness of and concern about oppressive systems. But she also concerns herself with representing the private feelings of contemporary transgender people who she is not genuinely trying to understand, and this is not fair to those individuals.

To speak about it as a modern matter: Leave transgender people alone. We did not invent sexism. Attempting to take away our genders does not make prejudice go away. It perpetuates it.

The Transsexual Empire is a screed. It does not correspond to the reality of transgender lives any more than Claudian's 4th-century screed *Against Eutropius* gives us information about what it was to be a eunuch.

Recommendation

This transsexual is capable of political consciousness, and here's one way in which I politicize my understanding of vilified eunuchs:

Screeds are a kind of fiction.

The twist: Sometimes, the villain is not the eunuch. Sometimes, the villain is the person who incorrectly tells you that you're a eunuch or that you don't exist. Sometimes, you spot the villain because they try to sell you a demonic, upside-down, unrecognizable version of your own story.

That is, if you, as a writer, misrepresent an entire gender by framing its members' personal and political consciousness as a series of catch-22s that make it impossible for you ever to view them as good people or to attempt to see them as they see themselves, *you* are playing the role of the villain. What you are doing is villainous because you are *scheming* to attack someone in an elaborate fashion for no good reason except your own obsession with them. Fortunately, that's a role you can stop playing at any time.

Janice Raymond may fret about a potential revival of the "political implications of historical eunuchism" as a tool for controlling women.[332] I think a real-life

---

[332] Raymond, p. 106.

revival of harems is unlikely, and I think our efforts might be more reasonably directed at considering the political implications of writing fictional eunuch villains, including the caricature she published in *The Transsexual Empire*. Fictional villains make some literature more fun to read, but the auras of these characters make our real lives harder.

From Eunuchs to Transgender People: A Genealogy

Raymond might have a point in calling eunuchs the "forerunners" of transgender women. It is not *always and necessarily* offensive (even if it is *usually* so) to draw a connection between different groups of people who have their testicles removed for one reason or another. You have to explain, though, why the detail is relevant and important, what the similarity might mean, and why you are calling it out. If your point is insightful and useful, it's less likely to hurt, offend, or misinform.

Another author recently argued a detailed case for perceiving a relationship between those two gender categories, at least in China. The way in which he explains it does not conflate those genders and experiences and makes it clear that there is no plausible, imminent risk of a historical backtrack to a system of politically enforced, involuntary castration.

Howard Chiang, in his 2018 book *After Eunuchs: Science, Medicine, and the Transformation of Sex in Modern China,* identifies a "genealogical relationship between the demise of eunuchism and the emergence of transsexuality in China."[333] (He uses the word "transsexuality," and therefore so will I in discussing

---

[333] Chiang, Introduction.

his point.) These genders are not the same. Eunuchs were not seen as women, and, though they were often seen as "social pariahs," some achieved great political power and were essentially "living right next to the epicenter of the Chinese empire." Modern transsexuals, on the other hand, usually want to live entirely as women and are "viewed as an extreme minority." While some eunuchs were voluntarily castrated, their motivations bore "zero resemblance" to the motivations of today's transsexuals.[334] Eunuchism was once "normative" in China but "lost its aura, meaning, and cultural significance." Today, transsexuality is the "afterlife of eunuchism."[335] While eunuchs and transsexuals may seem to have similar "body morphology" and their physical change served as "a cornerstone of their new social, cultural, and political identity,"[336] it's important to pay attention to the different meanings of these genders, given "shifting realms of scientific truth claims and geopolitics."[337]

Indeed, Chiang says, transsexualism in China is a "new ontological concept" and, like eunuchism, its "historicity is contingent rather than foundational or uncontestable."[338] That isn't to say that a gender means whatever any individual wishes it to mean, but rather that widely agreed-upon cultural meanings may change slowly over time. He notes, too, that the emergence of the idea of transsexualism was concurrent with (and apparently not in opposition to) ideas about feminism, including education reform and the end of the custom

---

[334] Chiang, "Conclusion: China Trans Formed."
[335] Chiang, chap. 1.
[336] Chiang, "Conclusion: China Trans Formed."
[337] Chiang, chap. 1.
[338] Chiang, chap. 1.

of breaking and binding young girls' feet.

The commonly cited reason for why eunuchism ended in China was the fall of the imperial system that employed large numbers of castrated men. Another major reason, as Chiang elaborates in his book, was the 20th-century understanding of sex, including the discovery of sex hormones and investigations into how hormones help make us what we are. By the early 20th century, in conversation with Western scientists, "Chinese biologists promoted a vision of sex dimorphism, which construed the bodily morphology and function of the two sexes as opposite, complementary, and fundamentally different."[339] This new medical understanding meant that the public began to see eunuchs no longer as a kind of man but as members of a third sex, and therefore it "eroded the very aura and possibility of their cultural existence" as people who had played a specific masculine role. Simultaneously, the increased technical knowledge of how to "manipulate sex...paved the way for the increasing visibility and political legitimacy of transsexuals."[340] Chiang says that in the 1950s "the Chinese term *'bianxingren'* carried almost none of the psychopathological connotations that distinguished its English counterpart, 'transsexual.'"[341]

You may not find this argument especially appealing, explanatory, or endorsable, or you may have no opinion about it at all. I bring it up here because I think its very existence—the fact that it was made at all, and that it was made in this way—reveals something important. It shows that it is possible to

---

[339] Chiang, "Introduction: Toward a Genealogy of Sex."
[340] Chiang, "Conclusion: China Trans Formed."
[341] Chiang, chap. 5.

discuss eunuchs and transgender people in the same book and to point out intersections and continuities between them while maintaining a neutral or positive attitude toward all the groups involved. *Having eunuchs in one's gender "ancestry" does not need to be inherently negative.* It does not mean that one is mutilated. It does not mean that one is anti-feminist. Eunuchs are part of our shared history. In one way or another, we are all descended from eunuchs, just as we are descended from everything and everyone who came before us. There are ways to discuss that part of gender history without fear and loathing and instead with curiosity and openness.

CHAPTER SEVEN
NOT EVIL ENOUGH

Ordinary crimes weren't going to suffice for this book. I chose to stick to unambiguously villainous characters and themes. The intensity of these characters means that sometimes they "come back," as a recently vanquished supernatural opponent in a horror movie suddenly sticks out its gnarled hand with its bloody fingernails in the final scene and the screen goes dark and the lights come back on.

As an example of characters I didn't include, there's "two or three" anonymous eunuchs in the Bible who throw Queen Jezebel out the window to her death when a rebel comes knocking. (2 Kings 9:33-35) It is not clear within the text whether the queen was truly wicked or simply penalized for being a powerful woman, how normal this kind of regicide was, nor how much premeditation went into this particular assassination.[342]

Nor did I include Ahab in Herman Melville's *Moby-Dick* (1851). Ahab's ivory prosthetic leg, as observed by David T. Mitchell and Sharon L. Snyder in *Narrative Prosthesis*, is said to have "'pierced his groin' on a Nantucket beach, [and] his incapacities—physical, sexual, and psychological—are all eventually chalked up to complications."[343] Ahab is stereotyped as an emblem of "insanity, [and] obsessive revenge" due to his disabilities,[344] but it's debated whether he is a eunuch.

Nor did I include the harem guard from the dream scene in Rabindranath Tagore's 1895 short story "Hungry Stones" *(Kshudhita Pashan)*. A man at a train station—a setting that places him in modern times—recounts a series of vivid dreams in which he feels himself pulled into Bengal palace life 250 years earlier. In his dream, a palace guard armed with an unsheathed sword twice prevents him from meeting a beautiful woman who cried out for "rescue." The guard in both instances is described as a eunuch, black, and "terrible." In the first appearance, the guard is only

---

[342] Janet Everhart writes: "Jezebel, like other powerful leaders in cultures where eunuchs surround royalty, was literally cast from power by perhaps once-loyal eunuchs....Scholars rarely consider the possibility that the eunuchs' willingness to throw Jezebel into the street might represent a prearrangement between Jehu and court officials in Jezreel." Everhart, Janet S. "Jezebel: Framed by Eunuchs?" *The Catholic Biblical Quarterly*, vol. 72, no. 4, 2010, pp. 688–698. *JSTOR*, JSTOR, www.jstor.org/stable/43726895. [Quote is from p. 697, 698.]
[343] David T. Mitchell and Sharon L. Snyder. *Narrative Prosthesis: Disability and the Dependencies of Discourse*. Ann Arbor: The University of Michigan Press, 2000. [Kindle, 2014.] p. 123.
[344] Mitchell and Snyder. P. 120.

dozing, but even so his presence triggers "a sudden dread [that] froze the blood in my heart."[345] The eunuch perceived as terrible hasn't actually done anything. The meaning of the story as a whole may center more on a reckoning with a political past which feels distant yet, like a ghostly nightmare, can never be fully exorcised.[346] The story isn't about evil eunuchs.

Nor did I include the sailor Oliver Andersen, who, as we are told by the unreliable narrator at the outset of Knut Hamsun's 1920 novel *The Women at the Pump*, is injured when a barrel of whale oil rolls on him, crushes his pelvis, and leads to the amputation of his leg and a seven-month hospitalization in a foreign country. He is "crippled," having become "a half-man, a kind of freak."[347] Finally returning home to his girlfriend in their small Norwegian town, Oliver marries her, and she bears five children. Oliver is dissatisfied with his life and eventually feels that "he was no longer a person."[348] He subjects his wife to an abusive "nightly tussle" that is vaguely described as involving, for example, "sweeping her up against the wall,"[349] but they live together nonetheless.

The nature of the accident in his youth, so similar to Ahab's in *Moby-Dick*, remains in question throughout the book. "But then," Oliver tells his friend, "it doesn't matter to you or anyone else whether

---

[345] Rabindranath Tagore. "The Hungry Stones." Translated by C. F. Andrews. Quoting pp. 11, 15.
http://www.fulltextarchive.com/pdfs/The-Hungry-Stones-And-Other-Stories.pdf (pp. 2-19) Accessed Sept. 18, 2018.
[346] Suvadip Sinha (2015) Ghostly Predicament, *Interventions*, 17:5, 728-743, DOI: 10.1080/1369801X.2014.984615
[347] Hamsun, chap. 1.
[348] Hamsun, chap. 15.
[349] Hamsun, chap. 8.

it was a barrel of whale oil or a derrick that did me in."[350] What matters to the other characters is that he cannot have been the biological father of his children. What matters to the readers is that, since we cannot trust what we have heard about his accident—even his doctor insists on seeing and touching him naked before acknowledging his castration that occurred decades earlier—we cannot trust what we hear about his abusive behavior, either. We know that "he did not remain entirely innocent and velvety of soul" and, although no crimes "came to light" publicly,[351] we remain unsure what crimes he may have committed.

> There is no one, of course, who doesn't keep a wary eye on him, who doesn't hide from him, twisted as he is, so signally mauled, an abomination to his fellow creatures. Can he expect anyone to look at him willingly? His pendulous obesity is appalling, his whole being repulsive, the way he hops along the street insufferable. He is incomplete even as an animal, a quadruped, and he is not merely a cripple, he is a hollowed-out cripple, an empty husk. Once he was a human being. Off he hobbles.[352]

To hammer home the point, if some Norwegians perceived people from the East as weak or inferior, he has become associated with that prejudice: "Oliver's fat and sterility made him an Oriental. But was he even that?"[353] His neighbors object to his disabilities, then, but that isn't his fault. His moral character should be

---

[350] Hamsun, chap. 8.
[351] Hamsun, chap. 22.
[352] Hamsun, chap. 31.
[353] Hamsun, chap. 31.

more at issue, but his character is shrouded in mystery. I have not considered him a villain.

Nor did I include Schahabarim, an important supporting character in Gustave Flaubert's 1862 novel *Salammbo*, set during the 3rd century BCE in North Africa. Schahabarim chose to be castrated to serve as the high priest of Tanit. He's described as having a "slanting skull," skin that appears "cold to the touch," eyes "like the lamps in a tomb," and a face "contracted in some eternal longing, some grief."[354] When the Carthaginians decide the goddess has become passé, Schahabarim tries to defect to another god—Moloch or Baal—but he is initially disqualified for being a eunuch. He does, however, finally manage to dress as a priest of Moloch and to wield their sacrificial knife, with which he exterminates a soldier. His victim is the Libyan soldier Matho, whose defection and trickery has caused great trouble for the Carthaginians, and who has just been tortured by executioners so that he appears "no longer human…completely red from top to bottom." Schahabarim carves out his still-beating heart, lifts it on the "golden spatula" and presents it as an offering to the sun.[355]

Schahabarim is not a villain. He had to make an unreasonably great sacrifice just to become a member of the clergy. Then, he lost his job as clergy and was unfairly disqualified from taking a similar job. He somehow managed to take that role anyway. He did not use his knife for evil, but rather used it to put a suffering man out of his misery.

You see, my provisional sympathy with royal

---

[354] Flaubert, p. 55.
[355] Flaubert, p. 282.

assassins, a hunter of a vulnerable marine species, armed guards in nightmares, a domestic abuser, and a practitioner of a dark cult has led me to understand why they—Oh, wait. This is exactly what people warned me would happen if I tried to understand the dark side. Now I'm defending defenestration, revenge-killing of animals, nightmares, spouse-beating, and human sacrifice! There it is, the unconquerable ghost of my own villainy, leaping out of my own body to throttle me with my mistakes. The horror movie of the shortcomings of my own ethical sense keeps making space for sequels.

A Game of Thrones

Lord Varys is probably the most famous eunuch in popular culture today. When readers first meet him in George R. R. Martin's series *A Song of Ice and Fire,* he is a silk-and-velvet-clad official in a medieval fantasy land who, we are told, repels another lord on some visceral level. Martin published the first installment of *A Song of Ice and Fire*—better known through its screen adaptation "Game of Thrones"—in 1996. As of 2018, five long novels have been published while an eager fan base awaits the final two promised volumes.

Varys is hairless and fat, powders his clammy hands, and perfumes his mouth with lilacs. He smirks and uses interjections like "dreadful."[356] He is known as a eunuch in a realm where castration is sometimes inflicted as punishment, a context that could prompt the question of whether he once committed some grave misdeed.

Worse is his behavior in the moments when it

---

[356] Martin, *A Game of Thrones,* p. 599.

matters most. Initially seeming to take Lord Eddard Stark's side in an argument over royal succession, Varys stands in silence when Eddard's head is demanded and Eddard's bodyguards are massacred. Was Varys complicit in the coup? Varys then privately recommends to Eddard that he deliver a false confession of treason in hopes of leniency for himself and his children. Eddard follows Varys' advice, but it does not go well for him, and he is immediately beheaded. Did Varys know this would happen?

Having nearly concluded *Painting Dragons,* Varys should seem familiar to you. He draws his life from a time-honored trope of eunuch villains. He is a schemer, that much is clear. He is not just a spy, but the boss of all spies, the "master of whisperers." His eyes and ears are everywhere, and everyone feeds him information. He admits that he is "sly and obsequious and without scruple" because those traits serve his job description.[357] He is nonviolent, perhaps mainly due to cowardice of physical combat, but he has managed to weaponize information.

Despite his creepiness, however, his villainy is in doubt. This means several things.

First, I excluded him from all the previous examples of eunuch villains this book. That's simply because he isn't obviously evil to me. The other fictional characters explored here in *Painting Dragons* are Varys' ancestors and cousins, but they are more evil than he.

Second, the uncertainty about his villainy is part of what makes his character riveting. He will not admit to being in anyone's pocket nor to serving any interest other than the good of the Realm. (He does, however,

---

[357] Martin, *A Game of Thrones,* p. 761.

encourage a few individuals to *believe* he is loyal to them, as their misplaced trust makes it easier for him to manipulate them.) It is difficult for readers to determine the truth about his agenda. Why does he scheme? Does he simply enjoy the game? Does he want to see anyone suffer? Or does he truly entertain the notion of serving a greater good? He can be as lethal as he wishes to be, so what is he planning and why? This holds readers' attention through thousands of pages of text (and years of television programming).

Third, the fact that his character appeals to millions of fans suggests that George R. R. Martin did something right. He invoked a nearly unavoidable stereotype and played off of it in a new way. That's one way to handle a stereotype in a way that is fresher and a little more positive.

CONCLUSION
MIRRORING MAGIC

Claudian's *In Eutropium* was described by a scholar as "the cruellest (and most entertaining) invective that has come down to us from the ancient world."[358] This is exactly the problem with vilification. It's cruel, but it's still *entertaining*. That's why people do it. That's why *we*, sometimes, on our less attractive days, are guilty of it. It's the sort of thing that might make us feel guilty even for being entertained by it, especially when we are aware of how it leverages and intensifies stereotypes of people who are seen as gender-deviant. We "call it out," in the sense of identifying a crime and attributing blame. But when we do this, sometimes we don't

---

[358] This comment inspired Jacqueline Long to write her 1996 book, *Claudian's In Eutropium: Or, How, When, and Why to Slander a Eunuch*. It's from Alan Cameron's essay "Claudian" printed in *Latin Literature of the Fourth Century*, ed. J. W. Binns (1974). New York: Routledge, 2014. p. 144.
https://books.google.com.co/books?id=x1zXAwAAQBAJ&pg=PA144&lpg=PA144 Accessed August 5, 2018.

inhibit it but rather "call it out" more, in the sense of emboldening it and coaxing it out of its closet.

Sometimes there's a valid reason for criticizing or mocking groups of people. Nonetheless, when people are "flattened into one-dimensional morality lessons," as Stephen Asma put it, the symbolism can cause problems if we ever meet those metaphorically flattened individuals in the flesh.[359] It's one thing to tell stories about abstract or imagined threats, and another to meet human beings very much like ourselves and discover that we must have functional interactions with them after having told embarrassing stories about them.

A person might identify with eunuchs for any number of reasons. He might have been born physically different, or chose to be different, or had something happen to him. She might occasionally pass as a man in public. They might have a nonbinary identity and use gender-neutral pronouns like "they/them" in reference to themselves. Maybe this person just has an affinity for people who are physically different or are treated as such.

And might someone identify with villains? Yes. That's at once darker and yet more common. We have to have a dark side so that we can renounce it. That dynamic is part of having a conscience. We couldn't claim to have a healthy, functioning conscience if our conscience had nothing to do all day. Recognizing villains and being secretly pleased and simultaneously repulsed by them is something everyone does.

If you decide to write a eunuch villain, you may simply presume that at least one reader will identify

---

[359] Asma, p. 76.

with him, but you don't need to predetermine or prejudge all of the reasons your reader might have for doing so. If the character is complex, he will offer multiple hooks to attract different readers.

Untying Your Story From Prejudice And Assumptions

Prejudice has common features in all eras. We tend to dehumanize and vilify anyone who is different, who challenges our assumptions, who breaks our binary categories and throws our systems out of whack. We know it is wrong and harmful to treat people as inhuman simply because they are different. Yet we do it. We keep making these systems that force people to be seen as different.

This book, *Painting Dragons,* revealed eunuch characters who were shown as villains in different places and times. It examined Roman and Byzantine eunuch officials portrayed in fiction and a later Western European screed against eunuch marriage; portrayals of reviled Ming dynasty eunuchs and a European farce set at the end of the Chinese imperial system; stories of Iran and Turkey and a fantasy land that resembles Persia; two similar tales of a traumatized Italian boy singer; recent novels about a child serial killer, a miniature vampire, and an aspiring demon; a modern screed against transgender people and a more sympathetic modern interpretation of how the Chinese concept of eunuchs evolved and made way for a concept of transgender identity; and novels in which the eunuch character is ambiguously villainous.

If you are writing a historical tale, you may feel more comfortable knowing what people historically believed about eunuchs and why they believed it, but that theory may not need to creep into your story. Seeing prejudice *today* (in feelings and in operation, in oneself and in others) may be enough to inform a story set in any time and place. Prejudice works pretty much the same everywhere. It's just something someone thinks they know or a rumor they start so they can feel in control.

One of the common features of prejudice is its general invalidity—that is, its factual and moral failings. When you write your story, you don't need to hypothesize that there are (somewhere out there) intellectually satisfying reasons to disapprove of eunuchs, and you don't need to set out to find them. You could just as readily hypothesize that such disapproval is usually unsound and that, if it is culturally pervasive or individually compelling, its impact is due to its appeal to emotions like fear, anger, and disgust.

Resisting assumptions takes some effort. The novelist Junot Diaz, interviewed in 2012, said that men must be "actively, consciously working against the gravitational pull of the culture" when they write women characters or their results will "predictably" disappoint their obligation to transcend cultural assumptions about women.[360] There is no other way to get the positive result than to make the effort. It will not happen accidentally, and whatever does happen accidentally will not be redeemed by *readers* on the basis that the *writer* felt that it was good.

Here's a place to start. When you write a eunuch narrative, you may want to change up a few things. Examples are:

---

[360] "'The Baseline Is, You Suck': Junot Diaz on Men Who Write About Women." Interviewed by Joe Fassler. *The Atlantic.* Sept. 12, 2012.

- Just because a boy was castrated with a knife does not mean the audience has to see the knife.
- Just because many eunuchs were servants, singers, or sex slaves doesn't mean *this* one has to be any of those things.
- Just because the eunuch wants revenge doesn't mean he needs to take up that quest.

Furthermore, just because a depiction is "realistic" (plausible or even common) doesn't mean it needs to be included in your story. Maybe your story wants a less common or even a slightly implausible character.

If you are in search of historically or medically accurate facts about eunuchs, it would be good to seek scholarly work on that specific time and place or on the specific medical condition or procedure that interests you. Having more factual knowledge is always useful, and it will definitely help you improve your fiction, as you will have better ideas about what information to include and what to exclude. As you learn more, you may find that you do not have to draw from the most shocking and frequently repeated accounts.

You have to do some research anyway, because all your characters need:

- A place and time.
- A social class, a race, a nationality, a language.
- A gender identity and sexuality (possibly flourishing, or possibly suppressed, damaged, ambiguous, or absent).
- A gender presentation that tends masculine,

feminine, recognizably third-gender such as eunuch, or less recognizably "other."
- A set of beliefs (religious or secular) that enable community with others.
- Private thoughts and a unique sense of self (tied, in some way, to all of the above).

A eunuch character will likely need:

- A history of whether he was born with an intersex condition or whether he suffered an illness or injury.
- A specific kind of damage sustained to specific parts of his body and an event or process by which the castration occurred.
- Another person who had some motivation to castrate him or to help him castrate himself.
- An environment that has particular social understandings and agreements about castration (even if the "understanding" is mostly ignorance and multiple "agreements" reveal themselves to conflict), including whether castration is understood as a disability.
- A private interpretation of his castration that is enabled by his overall worldview.
- Preferences and decisions about when to reveal personal details to other characters, unless all the information is already on the table to everyone all the time.

If you, as the writer, can answer these questions, it will strengthen the eunuch character. Even if you don't directly reveal the answers to the reader, the reader should be able to make informed guesses about your intention for how the character should be understood.

At a certain point, however, it may not be possible or desirable to try to reveal or understand any more about a character. The poet Cameron Awkward-Rich, asked in 2016 how they discuss sadness about racism and transphobia in their work, said that it's important to use literature to "catalog" the injuries, yet readers risk interpreting these themes in ways that "reinforce these systems rather than disrupt them." We might assume that the person is destined to feel sad and has no other possible way to live, or we might assume that empathizing with them through literature is sufficient replacement for correcting the problems in the real world.[361] Jos Charles, explaining one of her poetry collections, said in 2018 that other people's pain is often simply "unknowable" and that it may do them a "disservice" to try to package them in a "relatable or sympathetic" way to readers who can't authentically relate or sympathize because their lives are so dissimilar.[362] This means that your characters don't have to be excessively tragic, nor does their tragedy have to be overexplained.

As a reader or a writer, it's fine to accept that you have some distance from the fictional person you're writing about. When I find a character whose story resonates with me but who is significantly dissimilar to me, the experience feels like a fantasy "magic mirror" portal. I stand in front of a mirror. I begin to realize

---

[361] "Cameron Awkward-Rich: On Engaging With Trans Literary Tropes and Writing For the Future." Interviewed by H. Melt. *Lambda Literary.* June 8, 2016.
[362] "The Complicated Beauty of Jos Charles' Words." Interviewed by Molly Savard. *Shondaland.* Aug. 14, 2018.

that the person I'm seeing in the mirror is not me and that the overall picture in the mirror is not the real world. I touch the mirror. Reality goes wavy. My hand is in two worlds at the same time. I am apprehensive about entering the mirror and going all the way to the other side because I don't intend or need to become someone or something I'm not. I want to stay in the moment in which I'm experiencing two things at once. That's when I experience the "mythic distance" of seeing the archetype who represents me while, at the same time, I have no need to literally *be* him.

"It's not even the urge to fly or to be released from the bonds of gravity," writes Steven Church in *One With the Tiger*, analyzing the urge to jump off a cliff, "but instead to be suspended within them, to live, if only for a moment, in between action and consequence."[363] Church is discussing the sensation of *l'appel du vide*, the call of the void, the odd sensation of wanting to jump without having a suicidal intent. I see his words as another way of phrasing the moment in which I test the magic mirror. In this moment, I've started to act, but I can still take it back. I'm taking a big, imaginative risk. I want to see what my imagination does when I'm suspended between the constraint of being who I really am and the possibility of understanding a fictional character who is intimately unveiling before me. I want to imagine, if I briefly touched someone else and drew from his wisdom, into which reality would the mirror spit me? Would I lurch backward and come to understand myself as I really am, or if I would be sucked forward and change into something new and unrecognizable?

---

[363] Church, p. 101.

Who Are You as a Writer? Who's Your Reader?

Your story will have an impact in the world. Its impact will be determined in part by who reads it.

Who will read your book? No one can say exactly. Once you put it out there, you don't control who picks it up. It is certain that your identity will attract or repel some readers. That's unavoidable, but, depending on how you handle your identity, you can either tighten the constraints or broaden the invitations.

A reader's attitude and method influences what they will find inside a book, but what they find is also determined by what you, the writer, put on paper and make available to be found. You can't predict who will pick up the book and why it will interest them. As previously discussed, your fictional eunuch character might be of interest to a reader who is, himself, castrated, or to someone who isn't castrated but who is eager to read between the lines to satisfy a personal agenda or interest.

After reading this book, you may have new ideas about how to handle your eunuch villain. You may make a more radical decision that your eunuch won't be a villain or that your villain won't be a eunuch. It is ultimately up to you. I hope this exploration has helped you decide what magic you want to see in your mirror.

ACKNOWLEDGMENTS

Dominika Bednarska and freelance editors Helen Burroughs, Celeste Paed, and Emily Royalty-Bachelor provided valuable feedback on an early draft of this manuscript, and I am grateful for additional input from Sharon Annable, my father Marc Lieberman, and my husband Arturo Serrano. The cartoonist Andi Santagata created the haunting book cover. My publishing coach Robbie Samuels gave expert advice on bringing this into the world.

I appreciate my readers, too, for your time. If you liked *Painting Dragons* or learned something meaningful, please consider posting an online review or telling someone about the book. You are how the word gets out.

Thank you all.

ABOUT THE AUTHOR

Tucker Lieberman also published *Ten Past Noon: Focus and Fate at Forty* (2020), a biography of a New Yorker who tried to write a world history of eunuchs.

His bilingual poetry collection inspired by the Epic of Gilgamesh, *Enkidu is Dead and Not Dead / Enkidu está muerto y no lo está*, was a finalist for the Grayson Books poetry prize (2020).

He has written several memoirs. *Bad Fire* (2018, revised 2020) is about hallucination. "Crack Horse Race" is in *Letters for My Brothers: Transitional Wisdom in Retrospect*, an anthology nominated for a Lambda Literary award (2012). "Hearing Beneath the Surface: Crossing Gender Boundaries at the Ari Mikveh" is in *Balancing on the Mechitza: Transgender in Jewish Community*, an anthology that won a Lambda Literary award (2011).

He had a sex change when the Internet was dial-up, then became an early adopter of same-sex marriage and shortly afterward of same-sex divorce. He trained as a life coach at the Easton Mountain retreat center for gay men.

Originally from Boston, Massachusetts, he lives with the science fiction writer Arturo Serrano in Bogotá, Colombia.

WWW.TUCKERLIEBERMAN.COM

BIBLIOGRAPHY

Ancillon, Charles. *Eunuchism Display'd*. Translated by Robert Samber. London: Edmund Curll, 1718.

Asma, Stephen T. *On Monsters: An Unnatural History of Our Worst Fears*. Oxford: Oxford University Press, 2009.

Banks, Iain. *The Wasp Factory*. Simon & Schuster, 2013.

Brown, Dan. *The Lost Symbol*. New York: Doubleday, 2009.

Chiang, Howard. *After Eunuchs: Science, Medicine, and the Transformation of Sex in Modern China*. New York: Columbia University Press, 2018.

Church, Steven. *One With the Tiger: Sublime and Violent Encounters Between Humans and Animals*. Soft Skull Press, 2016.

Claudian. *Against Eutropius* (Vols. 1 and 2). Translated by Maurice Platnauer. Cambridge, Mass. And London: Loeb Classical Library, 1922.
Vol. 1:
http://penelope.uchicago.edu/Thayer/E/Roman/Texts/Claudian/In_Eutropium/1*.html
Vol. 2:
http://penelope.uchicago.edu/Thayer/E/Roman/Texts/Claudian/In_Eutropium/2*.html

Darmon, Pierre. *Damning the Innocent: A History of the*

Persecution of the Impotent in pre-Revolutionary France. New York: Viking, 1986.

Everhart, Janet S. "Jezebel: Framed by Eunuchs?" *The Catholic Biblical Quarterly* 72:4 (2010): 688–698. JSTOR, www.jstor.org/stable/43726895

Fassler, Joe, interviewer. "'The Baseline Is, You Suck': Junot Diaz on Men Who Write About Women." *The Atlantic.* Sept. 12, 2012. https://www.theatlantic.com/entertainment/archive/2012/09/the-baseline-is-you-suck-junot-diaz-on-men-who-write-about-women/262163/ Accessed August 30, 2018.

Ferguson, D. Andrew, Brian Jelke, Don Morgan, Mark Plemmons, and Jarrett Sylvestre. *Villain Design Handbook: Kingdoms of Kalamar.* Mundelein, Ill.: Kenzer and Company, 2002.

Flaubert, Gustave. *Salammbo.* Translated by A. J. Krailsheimer. England: Penguin, 1977.

Graves, Robert. *Count Belisarius.* RosettaBooks, 2014.

Hamsun, Knut. *The Women at the Pump.* Translation by Farrar, Straus & Giroux, Inc. Gyldendal Norsk Forlag, 2013.

Han, Jeremy. *The Prisoners of Fate.* Jeremy Han, 2015.

van der Hart, Onno, Ellert R. S. Nijenhuis, and Kathy Steele. *The Haunted Self: Structural Dissociation and the Treatment of Chronic Traumatization.* New York and London: W. W. Norton and Co., 2014.

Hegel, Robert E. "Conclusions: Judgments on the Ends of Times." David Der-wei Wang and Shang Wei, eds. *Dynastic Crisis and Cultural Innovation: From the Late Ming to the Late Qing and Beyond.* Harvard University Asia Center, 2005. p. 532. DOI: 10.2307/j.ctt1tg5hxm.20
https://pages.wustl.edu/files/pages/imce/hegel/h

egel_ends_of_times_0.pdf

Hill, John Spencer. *The Last Castrato.* New York: St. Martin's Press, 1995.

Howarth, Stephen. *The Koh-i-noor Diamond: The History and the Legend.* London: Quartet Books, 1980.

Kaplan, Matt. *The Science of Monsters: The Origins of the Creatures We Love to Fear.* Scribner, 2012.

Kelsey-Sugg, Anna. "Murderers or mentally ill: The problematic history of transgender characters on screen." Australian Broadcasting Corporation (ABC News), 15 August 2018. http://www.abc.net.au/news/2018-08-16/changing-media-representations-of-trans-people/10114402

Klosterman, Chuck. *I Wear the Black Hat: Grappling With Villains (Real and Imagined).* Scribner, 2013.

Koontz, Dean. *Frankenstein: Lost Souls.* New York: Bantam, 2010.

Kurlander, Eric. *Hitler's Monsters: A Supernatural History of the Third Reich.* New Haven and London: Yale University Press, 2017.

Lindqvist, John Ajvide. *Let Me In.* Translated by Ebba Segerberg. New York: Thomas Dunne, 2008.

Long, Jacqueline. *Claudian's In Eutropium: Or, How, When, and Why to Slander a Eunuch.* Chapel Hill and London: University of North Carolina Press, 1996.

Martin, George R. R. *A Game of Thrones: Book One of A Song of Ice and Fire.* New York: Bantam Spectra, 1996.

Martin, George R. R. *A Clash of Kings: Book Two of A Song of Ice and Fire.* New York: Bantam Spectra, 1999.

Martin, George R. R. *A Storm of Swords: Book Three of A Song of Ice and Fire.* New York: Bantam Spectra,

2000.

Martin, George R. R. *A Feast For Crows: Book Four of A Song of Ice and Fire.* New York: Bantam Spectra, 2005.

Martin, George R. R. *A Dance With Dragons: Book Five of A Song of Ice and Fire.* New York: Bantam Spectra, 2011.

McIntosh, Fiona. *Odalisque.* HarperCollins, 2009.

McIntosh, Fiona. *Emissary.* HarperCollins, 2009.

McIntosh, Fiona. *Goddess.* HarperCollins, 2009.

McMahon, Keith. "The Potent Eunuch: The Story of Wei Zhongxian," *Journal of Chinese Literature and Culture* 1 (November 2014): 1-2.
http://kmcmahon.faculty.ku.edu/pdf/McMahon-The-Potent-Eunuch.pdf

McNally, David. *Monsters of the Market: Zombies, Vampires and Global Capitalism.* Chicago: Haymarket, 2012.

Melt, H., interviewer. "Cameron Awkward-Rich: On Engaging With Trans Literary Tropes and Writing For the Future." *Lambda Literary.* June 8, 2016. https://www.lambdaliterary.org/interviews/06/08/cameron-awkward-rich-on-engaging-with-trans-literary-tropes-and-writing-for-the-future/ Accessed August 30, 2018.

Midgley, Mary. *Wickedness: A Philosophical Essay.* Taylor & Francis e-Library, 2003.

Mitchell, David T. and Sharon L. Snyder. *Narrative Prosthesis: Disability and the Dependencies of Discourse.* Ann Arbor: The University of Michigan Press, 2014.

Morier, James Justinian. *Zohrab, the Hostage.* (Vols. 1, 2, and 3.) London: Richard Bentley, New Burlington Street, 1832.

Pettit, Charles. *The Son of the Grand Eunuch.* Translator unknown. New York: Avon, 1949.

Piggot, John. *Persia: Ancient & Modern.* London: Henry S. King & Co, 1874.

Raymond, Janice G. *The Transsexual Empire: The Making of the She-Male.* New York and London: Teachers College Press, 1994.

Rodgers, Richard, Lorenz Hart, and Herbert Fields. "Chee-Chee." Adapted by Musicals Tonight, 2002.

Rodker, John. Personal correspondence to Ludmila Savitzsky. Sept. 13, 1937. John Rodker papers at the Harry Ransom Center, University of Texas, Austin. RLIN Record ID TXRC03-A15.

Sanchez, J. Wolf. The Last Castrato. Suchamedia, 2006.

Savard, Molly, interviewer. "The Complicated Beauty of Jos Charles' Words." *Shondaland.* Aug. 14, 2018. https://www.shondaland.com/inspire/books/a22541479/jos-charles-feeld-poetry-interview/ Accessed August 31, 2018.

Sedda, Anna and Gabriella Bottini. "Apotemnophilia, body integrity identity disorder or xenomelia? Psychiatric and neurologic etiologies face each other." *Neuropsychiatr Dis Treat.* 2014; 10: 1255–1265. 2014 Jul 7. doi: 10.2147/NDT.S53385 https://www.ncbi.nlm.nih.gov/pmc/articles/PMC4094630/

Shawl, Nisi and Cynthia Ward. *Writing the Other: A Practical Approach.* Seattle: Aqueduct Press, 2011.

Sinha, Suvadip. (2015) Ghostly Predicament, *Interventions,* 17:5, 728-743,
DOI: 10.1080/1369801X.2014.984615

Sykes, Sir Percy. *A History of Persia.* Volume 2. Chapter LXXIV, "The Founding of the Kajar Dynasty." Oxon, England: RoutledgeCurzon, 2004.

Tagore, Rabindranath. "The Hungry Stones." Translated by C. F. Andrews. Pages 2-19. Accessed Sept. 18, 2018. http://www.fulltextarchive.com/pdfs/The-Hungry-Stones-And-Other-Stories.pdf

Wheatley, Dennis. *The Eunuch of Stamboul.* Boston: Little, Brown, and Company, 1935.

Wu, H Laura. "Corpses on Display: Representations of Torture and Pain in the Wei Zhongxian Novels." *Ming Studies* 1 (2009): 42-55, http://dx.doi.org/10.1179/175975909X466435

www.ingramcontent.com/pod-product-compliance
Lightning Source LLC
Chambersburg PA
CBHW020256030426
42336CB00010B/787